JESUS
FACE-TO-FACE

Tales of fleeting personal encounters with
The Christ found in the New Testament Gospels

By

Greg Hadley

Copyright © 2011

Copyright © 2012 by Greg Hadley

All rights reserved. No part of this book may be reproduced, scanned or distributed in any printed or electronic form without permission. Please do not participate or encourage piracy of copyrighted materials in violation of the author's rights. Purchase only authorized editions.

Hadley, Greg [1934 -   ]
Jesus Face-to-Face / Greg Hadley—1st edition

ISBN: 1-4792-0752-7

Printed in the United States of America
First edition

OTHER BOOKS BY GREG HADLEY

Fundamentals of Baseball Umpiring - 1

Common Problems; Common Sense Solutions - 2

100 Everyday Epiphanies:
   Simple Events That Can Inspire Prayer

God's Words to My Heart

Aging: The Autumn Phase of Life
   How to navigate through the Golden Years
   with grace and fulfillment

Twilight Reflections
   Where the Elderly Find God

1 - In the National Baseball Hall of Fame, Cooperstown, New York

2 - Translated into Chinese for sale in Asia-Pacific region

Please visit our website for further information.
www.gbhadley.com

Dedication

To Sister Peter Mary McInnis, SNJM. Though small in stature, she has an enormous heart full of love for God and her neighbors. I have been blessed to have been loved by Sr. Peter Mary.

Table of Contents

FOREWORD I
PREFACE IV
JACOB, THE FATHER OF JOSEPH 1
KATARA, A CHILD BLESSED BY JESUS 4
JORAM, A RICH YOUNG MAN 8
SCHLOMO, OWNER OF LAST SUPPER HOUSE 14
BARABBAS, THE CRIMINAL 19
ANTONIAS, CAPTAIN OF THE GUARD 23
BENJAMIN, THE PARALYTIC 31
LEGION, THE POSSESSED MAN 35
DAN, THE MONEY CHANGER 40
JEHUDI, THE SCROLL ATTENDANT 45
SIMON, THE CYRENIAN 50
HILIEL, THE PHARISEE TESTING JESUS 55
ZEBEDEE, FATHER OF JAMES AND JOHN 62
SIMON THE LEPER 67
PERES, THE SERVANT MAID 74
NAOMI, PETER'S MOTHER-IN-LAW 83
TELES, THE MAN WITH A WITHERED HAND 92
ASHSAH, THE WOMAN WITH HEMORRHAGES 100
ISAAC, A SHEPHERD AT BETHEHEM 108
MILCAH, A GIRL BROUGHT TO LIFE 116
BARUCH – THE WINE STEWARD AT CANA 124
SARAI – THE POOR WIDOW 132

HELENA, THE SYROPHOENICIAN WOMAN	137
BARTIMAEUS, THE BLIND BEGGAR	144
MALCHUS, THE HIGH PRIEST'S SERVANT	151
JOHN, THE BOY WITH THE LOAVES AND FISH	159
CAIUS, A CENTURION AND HIS SLAVE	166
CALEB, AND HIS POSSESED SON, GAD	174
MOSHA, THE WOMAN CAUGHT IN ADULTERY	180
JOBAL, THE CRIPPLED MAN AT BETHESDA	187
MAXIS, WHO MADE THE CROWN OF THORNS	193
REUBEN, MARTHA AND THEIR BLIND SON, SHEM	199
ABOUT THE AUTHOR	207

FOREWORD

Jeremiah 17: 14 – "Heal me and I will be healed; save me and I will be saved, for you are the one I praise."

My father-in-law, the author of this book, asked me to write this Foreword because I was blessed only months ago with a dramatic physical healing. He felt my contribution would be meaningful since many of the stories herein are about miraculous cures. My story seems insignificant compared to those in this book although I closely identify with many of the characters described in these pages. Throughout this book, you will discover wondrous tales of many anonymous people whose spiritual, emotional, psychological—and physical—wounds were healed. Truly, our God provides restorative blessings of many kinds to those who are suffering from a variety of illnesses.

Some might say my healing did not come directly from the Great Physician himself. I disagree with that. I am reminded of Jesus' words in John 5: 17: "My Father is always at work to this very day, and I too am working." I am convinced He brought healing to me by working through ordinary people.

My miraculous improvement came after thirty-five years of what is described in Leviticus as a "defiling skin disease." Decades of medical care from top specialists did little to help me. Over the last five years my health and quality of life declined significantly. I could barely get dressed or put on shoes. My raw and bleeding hands were a torment. Frequently I was frantic and despairing. I was worried about what lay ahead for me. Yet, the worst was still to come.

Over a period of six months I lost most of my hair. I would like to tell you I was faithful, accepting, brave and optimistic. In truth, I became depressed, self-pitying, and nearly a recluse despite a busy and demanding life with a husband and four school-age children. My lowest point came when I recognized I was close to being labeled as "disabled."

The loss of my hair meant it was no longer possible to hide my condition. I was forced to become more open about my health, the struggles it imposed upon me and my worries. I continued to pray without ceasing, and many others joined in praying for me too.

I believe all these prayers touched the Lord's heart. His merciful response helped me to form a healing plan that became my own personal miracle. After extensive investigation, I decided to attend an eight-day program at a specialty hospital in Denver. Not only did I find healing there but also saw the face of Jesus in the team of medical personnel who treated me. There were doctors who untangled the genetic network that was causing my overlapping conditions. There were nurses whose hands bathed, medicated and soothed my inflamed, infected physical shell. There was a pharmacist who filled my prescriptions after hours. There were current and former patients who encouraged me and taught me about the virtue of hope. I saw the loving, gentle face of Jesus in all those people who helped me recover. Like many described in this book, I encountered Jesus face-to-face.

While I did not meet them personally, I thank God for the benefactors who donated the funds to build the wing of the hospital where I was treated. What generous and loving people they must be!

We are promised in Romans 8: 28, "God uses all for the good of those who love Him." He used my suffering for my good and well as for His glory. He traded my sackcloth for clothes of joy.

My physical healing is proof that miraculous cures were not confined to biblical times. As you read this book you may think it was only during the time that Jesus walked this earth that these wondrous events took place. While we cannot see or touch him physically, I know that He still dwells within me. His abundant grace is available to you and me just as it was to those described in this book. As you read these pages, I hope and pray that you also encounter Jesus face-to-face. When you do, ask for his loving and healing touch. I am sure He is willing to help you as He has helped me.

Suzanne Hoff Hadley
Manhattan Beach, California

PREFACE

The New Testament Gospels of Matthew, Mark, Luke and John are replete with stories about people having brief personal encounters with Jesus. Some of these reported incidents are so fleeting that the people involved are unnamed. In the blink of an eye and with but a handful of words, these folks become bit players in the salvation play where Jesus is the central figure.

Who were these people, really? What occurred in their lives that qualified them for inclusion in sacred scripture? Can you imagine how they might have been affected by seeing Jesus and speaking with him face-to-face? Obviously, they all had stories; wouldn't it be fascinating to know what their stories were? Alas, except for a few historical snippets, we know very little about these people. We can only use our imagination to create plausible tales detailing the circumstances that led to the encounter, build on scriptural accounts, study various commentaries and expand what few words describe the meeting event. Next, one may speculate about the hours, days and months that followed. Were those uninterested in Jesus inspired by meeting him? Did skeptics become believers? Were hearts touched? Lives changed? Did some encounters result in tragic missed opportunities? Even great scholars cannot tell us about all the emotions or the detailed circumstances surrounding these scriptural episodes. Those barriers to knowledge should not impede us. We can create compelling stories about the people that encountered Jesus, provided we are careful to observe historical accuracy, as we know it, and honor customs and traditions of that time.

So, that is what this book is all about. You will find thirty-two mostly fictional tales about men, women and children who spoke to Jesus during his life upon this earth. Where characters are not identified in scripture, I have named them to personalize their story. Each account provides the reader with some background about the person such as where he or she lived, what they did for a living, how they came to know about Jesus, the actual circumstances of the meeting and what happened afterward. You will read about Ashsah, the woman afflicted with hemorrhages; Joram, a rich young man who loved his possessions; Schlomo, the man who owned the building where the Last Supper was held; Dan, one of the money changers in the temple; Jehudi; the scroll attendant in the Nazareth temple, and many more.

You will also read more details about familiar characters such as Barabbas, Simon the Cyrenian, blind Bartimaeus, Simon the leper, Peter's mother-in-law and Zebedee, the father of the Apostles James and John.

Finally, each story ends with a contemporary reflection. How might each of us have responded to a physical meeting with Jesus? Two thousand years later, are there lessons that we can learn from these stories that apply to our lives today? Even though many of us may feel quite anonymous spiritually in a world containing four billion people, our faith informs us that God lives within our souls and loves each one of us unconditionally just as we are. We have the great benefit of hindsight. We *know* how the gospel stories turned out. Those who saw Jesus face-to-face in our tales weren't so well informed about what was really happening. As we try to place ourselves in their positions, we can look for ways to project these encounters into our own daily struggles, problems and circumstances. Perhaps the fictional accounts can help us make our current lives more meaningful and manageable.

The spirit of this book is found in the Gospel of John, Chapter 21 verse 25 where we read: *"There are also many other things that Jesus did, but if these were to be described individually, I do not think the whole world would contain the books that would be written."* While clearly acknowledging that the stories presented are mostly fictional, I believe they are also credible. The circumstances of daily living and the modes of communication today are dramatically different from those during Jesus' time on earth. In spite of that, we should acknowledge that we are much the same as the people who encountered Jesus physically. And so, it might be wise to immerse ourselves in these brief little tales to determine if we can identify with the characters described. One can imagine that there were hundreds, perhaps thousands, of similar incidents that have never been recorded. Maybe you can think of a situation that involves yourself, transported back in time, walking alongside Jesus and hearing him speak. What would you have said to him? How do you think he might have affected you? Would his radical call to look differently at God, your neighbor and how you must serve others have left you skeptical…or a devoted follower? I hope this book gives you a desire to break the contemporary chains of *groupthink* and reexamine your personal relationship with Jesus the Christ, fully human and fully divine.

Writing a book like this is lonely work. But, many people have encouraged and supported me during the time these stories were being written. There are so many who have loved and assisted me, I cannot acknowledge them all by name lest I leave someone important off the list. My heartfelt thanks to all who have been so kind to me as I traveled along this journey.

I am especially grateful to Suzanne Hoff Hadley who wrote the Foreword. Suzanne, my beloved daughter-in-law, is a person of deep faith and trust in God. The Foreword she has written is a great testament to her love of her Creator. She is a wonderful example of one tested in fire like refiner's gold. The healing she has experienced is a verifiable miracle, at least to me.

One character in this book is especially significant to me. Simon of Cyrene was called to assist Jesus in a most intimate way even though he was a total stranger. God picked Simon—just as He picked you and me—to do something important in life to help another. Have you figured out what you have been called to do? Have you done it yet? Personally, I am still trying to determine what I have been called to do.

This book has been written for Christian believers. Whether you are Catholic or Protestant, I feel sure you will find stories and reflections that resonate with you. I hope you enjoy reading these stories. I have gained great pleasure producing them. Hopefully, you and I can walk together on our salvation journey leading to our final glory when we will encounter Jesus face-to-face.

JACOB, THE FATHER OF JOSEPH
Matthew 1: 16

Every father wants the best for his children. That's why I was so pleased when my son, Joseph, told me that he was going to take Mary for his wife. She was well known—and very well liked—in our little town of Nazareth. Mary appeared to be a gentle soul who was full of love and compassion for her family, friends and neighbors. She seemed to be forever helping others by cooking, sewing, babysitting children or caring for someone who was sick. She was also a very lovely girl with an inviting smile and beautiful dark brown eyes. I did think she might be a little young to marry but she had a maturity about her that made her seem quite grown up. And, if I do say so myself, Joseph was a pretty good "catch" for some young woman. He never went through a wild or rebellious period as a teenager. He was always quite faithful to his religious studies and was active in the local temple so I never felt I had to worry about his ethics, prayer life or relationship with God. Joseph was also a very hard worker and has done a good job of establishing his carpentry and woodworking business. His client list is long and he receives good references from all he has served with his products and services. Yes, Joseph makes me proud and has been a very good son. I was sure he would turn out to be a loving, protective husband and father.

Mary and Joseph insisted upon a quiet, low-key wedding. They picked a day that turned out to be absolutely beautiful. The deep blue skies were dotted with small, puffy white clouds and the temperature was very mild and pleasant. In the weeks before the wedding, there was some rather nasty gossip about Mary by some of our village busybodies. Frankly, I was getting concerned about what was being said. But Joseph came to me one day and told me not to be worried; everything was OK and he was sure the Lord God was blessing his marriage to Mary. That was good enough for me; I loved and trusted Joseph completely. He would never tell me anything but the truth.

You know how busy young couples are these days. I didn't see them too often but once in awhile we would have dinner together. It wasn't long before Mary was showing her pregnancy. Towards the end of the year we were all on our way to our ancestral home, Bethlehem, to participate in the census that the Romans had decreed. While we were there, Mary and Joseph had a son whom they named Jesus. For some reason, there was a lot of excitement around his birth. If you can believe it, I was told that some local shepherds came down out of the nearby hills to visit Joseph's new son because some angel told them to. The stories one hears! And then the whole community was abuzz when we learned that a caravan from the east, headed by three noblemen, stopped by Mary and Joseph's home to present some very valuable and beautiful gifts to Jesus. None of us could figure out what was going on. What could have possibly prompted the nobles to do something like that? Naturally, I was pleased that my grandson received such unusual attention, but I was puzzled and, frankly, could not understand the meaning of this event.

That murderous Herod was told a new King of Israel had been born. From his evil heart came the command to kill every boy baby under two years old. This frightening prospect drove Joseph to take Mary and Jesus and escape to Egypt. I missed them so when they were gone. Jewish tradition tells us that "this, too, shall pass" and it wasn't long before Herod was dead. Feeling safe, Joseph brought his family back to Nazareth. It was great to see them!

Jesus was growing so quickly! What a handsome young man he had become. Once in awhile, he would come to visit me. You can imagine what a proud grandfather I was. I loved this boy as I did all my grandchildren but there was something very special about him. He exuded an inner glow as if he possessed a special gift—I could tell he was unique. We would talk for hours and, instead of my being the teacher as grandfather, I somehow felt that I was the one who was learning and being taught. It was a strange but very comfortable feeling. I could sense that I was in the presence of a child destined for greatness.

Imagine yourself as a parent or grandparent. We are proud of our children and grandchildren, but we also worry about the choices they make. Prayers aren't always answered the way we hoped. Young people get into jams and tight places that they can only escape through their own efforts. We feel hopeless and impotent, wanting to lend a hand but unable to do so. How do you deal with this situation? Should we turn over our offspring to God, asking Him to protect and guide these youngsters as they deal with their problems? Hopefully, they will come out the other side as stronger and wiser people. It is important for us to let go and let God. It's our best strategy.

Greg Hadley

KATARA, A CHILD BLESSED BY JESUS
Mt. 18: 1-5

I am going to tell you a story that happened ten years ago. It's about an experience I had when I was eight years old. Looking back now, as a wife and mother, the episode was life changing for me and, in some ways, for my entire family. First, I need to give you a little context about what was happening with my family and me a decade ago.

Children don't always understand many details about their family's situation. My sister and I probably believed our lives were pretty normal since they looked similar to those of our relatives, friends and neighbors. Now that I am older, I think our family was really struggling materially, emotionally and spiritually. My father was not a bad man. I mean, he rarely used physical punishment on us and I never saw any abuse of my mother. But he was also quite distant and showed little love towards any of us. Without being unkind, I must also describe him as un-ambitious and possessing limited skills and talents. Our financial situation was often precarious since father had a hard time finding and retaining work. He was also unenthused about religious activities in the local temple so none of us experienced a religious component to our daily lives. I really felt left out because most of my friends were very involved in temple activities.

Our hardscrabble existence kept us somewhat isolated from the rest of our community. We were seldom invited to community events and did not participate in the normal temple activities. As I said, children are not always tuned in to situations like this but, as I grew older, I did feel a little isolated. For example, we were probably the last family to hear about the young Rabbi, Jesus, who was traveling around the region preaching. Since I was so young then and without even basic religious training I had no way of understanding his message. I did overhear adults saying that his ideas were quite radical compared to what was taught in our own temple. Was that good or bad? Threatening or reassuring? I had no way of knowing at age eight. Even my passive father began picking up on the Jesus rumors and became surprisingly animated when he learned about parts of Jesus' message. I heard him say to my mother, I would like to see this Rabbi and hear what he has to say. If he ever comes to our region, we should arrange to do that.

One day, a neighbor boy came running down the street crying out, Rabbi Jesus is here! Rabbi Jesus is here! Heads popped out of windows and doors seeking verification. Yes, the boy exclaimed, Jesus is right on the edge of town—now! My mother, father and I all quickly left our home and joined a stream of people heading towards the place where Jesus was speaking. The village was small; we arrived to find a large group of people gathered around Jesus. I was very excited to see him! He was so...*beautiful*! I don't think I had ever thought that way about an adult male before. He was tall, had handsome features, brown hair and penetrating dark brown eyes. I also noticed his hands; they were expressive as he spoke. His voice was rich and authoritative. I was enthralled! As he addressed the crowd, his eyes landed on our family group. He smiled and said to my father, my friend, you and your family are welcome here. You have a lovely little daughter. Focusing on me Jesus said, what is your name, little girl? Blushing and feeling very self-conscious, I whispered, Katara. Nearby was a large rock on the side of the road. To my father Jesus said, may I hold her? Of course, my father mumbled. Jesus extended his arms and lifted me up while moving to the rock to sit down. He sat me on his knee. I felt comfortable and safe as he continued speaking to the throng. I even put my head on his chest as his arm cradled me and his hand rested lightly on my shoulder. He then paused for a moment; in silence, he glanced around the group of people. Finally, Jesus said, unless each of you changes and becomes like a little child—he pointed to me—you will not enter the kingdom of heaven. Humble yourselves, as this child is humble. And if you care for, nurture, and love a child like this you will be especially blessed by God.

That exquisite encounter with Jesus the Christ happened ten years ago. I will never forget one moment of the brief time he held me on his lap. Love and kindness exuded from him and I feel his gentle touch even now. I was ten when I heard about the terrible days when he was tortured, crucified and died. But my despair turned to hope, then joy, when I heard the stories of his resurrection from the dead and all the wonderful events that have occurred since. My meeting with Jesus also profoundly affected my father and mother. They both experienced a conversion and began leading lives full of love, hope, joy and peace. Now, a mature woman, I am fully committed to The Way as taught by Jesus and his apostles. In my heart I believe Jesus is the Christ who opened the gates of heaven for me through his death and resurrection. Lord Jesus, guide me and my family to everlasting life with you in Paradise. Amen.

In today's culture, we often hear the call to simplify our lives. Everyday life is so cluttered with material things that we have come to rely on for our existence and pleasure. Books have been written about how to rid yourself of everything that makes life more complicated and stressful. It is easy to see why this idea may be catching on. Everywhere we look we see people with earphones connected to iPod music devices while they scan their "smart" phones for the latest text message or tweet from a friend. And yet, this infatuation with technological materialism has not brought communities closer together or improved human communication. Many are connected, but still lonely. It is said that we can more richly experience life when we are detached from it. Scholars have examined communities of religious women and men who live simple, even monastic, lives. Those studied often profess deep happiness with life and feel a sense of peace because they can savor their daily existence with a perspective not filtered through materialism.

Katara certainly lived simply. While her life was imposed on her—not chosen—she still was able to react to a specific event with personal intensity. Snuggling in the arms of Jesus apparently changed her life forever. While you and I cannot physically embrace our God, we can discard all the clutter around us and become closer to him spiritually, intellectually and emotionally. Do you think you might be happier and more content if you felt God in your life more fully? Is it possible that we have become distracted from God's presence because we are so encumbered with "stuff" and "things?" Perhaps we should consider how to rid ourselves of all the unnecessary litter that blocks our path to a deep relationship with God. What do you think?

Greg Hadley

JORAM, A RICH YOUNG MAN
Mt. 19: 16-22
Mk. 10: 17-22

I must be honest with you. I live a life of great privilege. My grandfather and father before me were very successful merchants trading in spices, cloth, oil and precious metals like gold and silver. I cannot remember a day in my life when I was denied any material thing I needed—or wanted. We always lived in spacious, beautiful houses surrounded by tall, thick walls for our personal security. There were servants to care for our every need. They did whatever the family required—cooking, washing clothes, serving meals, cleaning the house, tending the gardens, hauling water and caring for our household animals. In spite of this opulent wealth, our parents tried to raise us with good values. We were taught to be respectful and courteous to all of the servants because they are God's children just as we are. My brother and I were also required to go to the temple each week on the Sabbath plus the religious studies school conducted during the week. Although we were considered to be very wealthy, my father also instructed us never to lord it over anyone less fortunate than we were. He practiced the life he preached; he was very generous in giving to the poor, sick and those facing hard times. Those who served our needs were justly paid for their service. Father often told us the story of Job, reminding us that our wealth came from God and he could take it away from us as quickly as he gave it to us. Therefore, as I grew to maturity, I had the intellectual disposition to understand that God's hand is present in everyone's life. If you happened to be wealthy and prosperous, that was a blessing from God. Be grateful and also be generous to those not so greatly blessed.

I wish I had inherited my Father's character. I cannot deny my strong attachment to riches and all the material comfort and pleasure wealth brings. Abba has this wonderful balance in his life. He is nonchalant about money, using it freely for himself and his family. He is equally quick to help those who find themselves in dire straits. I don't resent his generosity but, frankly, sharing my resources with others is not easy for me. I console myself with the fact that I diligently lead a moral and productive life, dealing with everyone honestly and fairly while seeking a prayerful relationship with God Almighty. Might I do better? Well, I'm sure I could.

I had traveled to several places to hear the young, new prophet named Jesus of Nazareth. His message to the people was quite different from what we heard in temple. Instead of preaching about strict adherence to Torah laws, he spoke more about loving your neighbor and your enemies, turning you cheek to those who attack you and many other things that differed from our upbringing. And yet, he was attracting increasingly large crowds to hear him preach. Although I had not personally witnessed it, many reported seeing Jesus cure the sick, lame and lepers and even raise some people from the dead. Amazing stories if they were true! Each time I happened to hear him, I was more impressed with his message and his personal charisma.

The next time I saw Jesus was at a small event. I had been following him long enough that he knew me by sight. When I came near him, he smiled and said, it is good to see you again. I have noticed you before and I'm pleased you continue coming to hear me preach. He extended his hand; I felt honored to be singled out for his individual welcome. His greeting to me was genuinely warm; I felt very engaged with him personally for the first time. After lingering over our exchange for an extended moment, he turned back to the others who were crowding around him and began to preach. He spoke movingly about the kingdom of heaven. Jesus said that that all men and women must cooperate with God's grace and do everything possible to enter eternal life in God's favor. I was so touched by his words that I broke through the throng and stood directly in front of Jesus. We were mere inches apart. I sensed his feelings of filial love toward me as any two brothers might experience. I wanted to possess this eternal life that Jesus spoke of; hearing his words made me desire it more than anything in my life. Looking deeply into Jesus' warm eyes, I said to him, teacher, what must I do to gain eternal life? He hesitated briefly as our eyes continued locked together. Then, Jesus said softly to me, you know the commandments, Joram. You shall not kill; you shall not commit sins of the flesh; you shall not steal; you shall not bear false witness; you shall not defraud; honor your father and mother; all of these and those given to us through Moses and the prophets. That, Joram, is what you must do to gain eternal life. But, teacher, I said, all of these things I have observed from my youth. Yet, I still have this feeling that I cannot claim eternal life. What else am I lacking so that I can gain this important prize? Jesus paused and took a deep breath. He reached out his right arm and placed his hand on my left shoulder. Looking at me with obvious love, he said quietly to me, Joram, you are lacking only one thing. Go, sell what you have, give the proceeds to the poor and you will have treasure in heaven. After you have done this, then come and follow me.

These words felt like scalding water poured on my soul. My face was burning red while tears welled up in my eyes. My body was rigid, my fists clenched into tight balls. Though I was silent, my mind raced to form a response to Jesus. I thought, why did he insist that I get rid of my possessions? They are so important to me, to my well-being, to my self-image, to my life style. I am willing and able to follow all the commandments but, oh, Jesus, you have exacted a terrible price from me for eternal life. As my mind raced I was searching Jesus' eyes and face for some reprieve, however small, from this final requirement. I could not find a single caveat. In distress, I finally broke our mutual gaze, looked down to the ground, turned and walked slowly away from Jesus. I felt like an insect, desperately skittering away from a huge predator. I was heartsick and tormented with guilt, experiencing tortuous emotions. The next few weeks of my life were spent in spiritual turmoil as I agonizingly relived Jesus' call to dispose of my riches and follow him. I found myself both hating Jesus and loving him at the same time. Was I the only person on earth who had rejected a direct call from Jesus? My existence had become a miserable ordeal.

Then, tragedy struck. Our father died very suddenly leaving our family business and financial situation in disarray. My siblings and I began vicious squabbling about our inheritance and we spent much time in front of the local judge fighting for our share of father's estate. Without him at the helm, the business was quickly collapsing, thus jeopardizing the financial future for the whole family. How ironic, I thought bitterly. Jesus told me to dispose of my wealth and follow him. The first part of that command was being taken care of for me without my cooperation and against my will.

My life of affluence had quickly become one of deprivation. No more servants, sumptuous food, fine clothes, lavish parties with friends or comfortable living quarters. I had been rich; now I was poor, struggling to eke out an existence by taking any job I could find. Hearkening back to my father's stories, I likened myself to a modern day Job with one exception. Job's status and wealth had been restored in the end. I knew my life was not to have such a happy conclusion. My riches had been a millstone around my neck. They had dragged me down into the abyss.

Greg Hadley

It is an unfortunate fact that most of us give what is left over to charity. We pay ourselves first by making sure the mortgage is covered, there is enough for school tuition, all car payments and utility bills are paid, grocery shopping and meals out are provided for and all the little, but important, items are budgeted for as well. After all this is accomplished, there may be some funds left over. Part of this remainder goes to charity...our church, our university, perhaps a local shelter for battered women or something similar. We hear about neighbors who tithe to their church. How can they possibly do that? Like Joram, many of us have a trust issue with God. We faithfully try to be good people, keeping all the commandments, going to church on Sunday and following the Golden Rule in our dealings with others. But money? No thank you, God, I'll take care of that issue myself. The problem is that every material thing we have—everything—is a gift from God. There is nothing we have done to earn these material blessings—nothing. After all, you could have been born in the most impoverished slum in Calcutta, India instead of a prosperous place like this. But, we kid ourselves and believe the story that only through our intelligence, ambition and hard work has our wealth been created. We earned it and we'll decide how it is to be used. It is too risky to turn this over to God; he might ask us to do something that does not fit our current plans. What we fail to understand is the impossibility to be more generous than God. So, instead of giving to God's work what is left over, we should pay him first. We should also work on our trust and to let God into our lives.

Will God ask you or me to sell everything, give the proceeds to the poor and then come and follow him? We will probably not be offered such a stark choice. But, I do believe God is calling us to reorder our priorities. First, we must work to develop a deep spirit of thanks for the many blessings we have been given as pure gifts from God. Second, we need to trust God more, being willing to take actions that may not appear to be in our self interest but that promote the kingdom of God here on earth. Finally, we must resist the relentless secular pressure to become slaves of consumerism. God does hear our prayers. Ask him for the grace you need to be truly thankful, Have a generous spirit and be inoculated against the pervasive indifference to materialism.

SCHLOMO, OWNER OF LAST SUPPER HOUSE
Mt. 26: 17-19

Most of my business friends, family and neighbors spend a lot of time talking about the current state of affairs in and around Jerusalem. First, I hear folks complaining about how brutal the Romans are, their completely arbitrary and unfair taxation and the ways they repress our religious liberties. Some continually plot how they might overthrow these foreign oppressors and reclaim the country for themselves. Others find our Jewish civic leaders to be inept and cowardly, always bowing and scraping to the Romans while trying to feather their own nests through cooperation with the occupiers. Throw in all those who hold strong religious beliefs, especially the ones who are promoting the latest so-called prophet on the scene, some man named Jesus. These political and religious rants from all sides have turned out to be a national pastime. It is like the weather; everyone talks about it but nothing changes the situation. It seems all one hears around town is the whispered whining and complaints of disgruntled conspiratorial small groups of people gathered in the alleys and shadows of the city. Politics! I am sick of it! I don't care and have no interest in the subject. Romans, Jews and religious zealots…all of them turn me off.

Actually, my life is totally focused on acquiring more real property and making as much money as I can. Let the Romans tax; I know how to avoid the most confiscatory of their levies. The Jewish leaders? All they are interested in is how many angels live on the head of a pin. As to prophets and proclaimed Messiahs, who cares? How does any of that change my life in any way? I work to accumulate wealth. I do this by buying up as many houses and buildings as I can. Then I rent these spaces at high prices and turn a tidy profit. I live well, dress in fine clothes, eat the best foods available and make sure that every earthly pleasure is available to me. All of those with their lofty ambitions for a Jewish state or some religious savior are fools, in my opinion. I believe you only live once so every effort should be made to garner wealth and live a life of luxury. Why not? When you die, you die...that's it. Why go to your grave regretting that you missed out on all life has to offer?

Passover is a good time for my business. Many visitors crowd into Jerusalem looking for places to stay or accommodations for their Passover meals. I go to the temple area with a sign that says: Spaces For Rent. People often gather around me and I make deals right on the spot. I'm not ashamed to say that I get premium prices because I have so many diverse units available to rent. This day near the temple was an unusually large group of people. In the center of this throng was a youthful preacher. When I asked who this young man was, I was told he was Jesus, the latest "Messiah of the month." As I got nearer, I could hear him speaking about love, caring for the poor and putting your neighbor equal to yourself. What garbage, I thought. The world only rewards those who put themselves first. Let the neighbor take care of himself...I'm too busy and don't care. I could not help being drawn into the group around Jesus. I give him credit; he was very articulate and persuasive with his preaching. Suddenly, his eyes fell on me. He said, Schlomo, (I don't know how he knew my name) I feel my words are not resonating in your heart. He continued, please think about what I have said. Later on, you may find that you will be touched by what you have heard. Perhaps you may even change the way you think about your life. He looked at me in a kindly way, I thought. I was uncomfortable and had an uneasy feeling he knew the concepts I embrace about living my life. I wanted to escape the crowd and be back to my business. As I turned to leave, I felt a hand on my shoulder. I swung around and was face-to-face with Jesus who was touching me. Schlomo, he said gently, I may have need for some of your space soon. My friends will contact you about arrangements. With that, he turned back to the crowd and continued his discussion with them. As I departed, I did not like the way I felt. My mind was racing and my previously firm convictions were suddenly confused and left me in turmoil. Who was this man, I thought angrily. By what right does he have to suggest how my life should be conducted? I continued to think about this Jesus as I arranged rental transactions with many visitors. Yes, business was very good indeed. Why, then, did I feel so upset and conflicted by this brief encounter with the man named Jesus?

Passover arrived. My inventory of space to rent was almost filled. Surprisingly, one very nice, well appointed upstairs room had not yet been taken. I wasn't worried; some well-to-do visitor will snatch up the unit before day's end, I was confident. The place was perfect for a Passover meal. The room contained a long table that could accommodate about twenty people. There was a kitchen alcove at the end of the room that was nicely stocked with table settings and cooking utensils. I will surely be able to take advantage of someone who had not planned ahead. They will be forced to come to me in the end; I was the largest landlord in the city.

At mid-morning on Passover, I happened to be near my remaining rental unit. I was heading to the bank to make a large deposit of the money I had collected in the last few days. I insist that all rent is payable in advance; there are no exceptions to that rule. As I hurried down the busy street, two men approached me. I recognized them; they had been with Jesus yesterday in the temple. Perhaps they are followers of his, I thought idly. As I reached them, they stopped and said, Schlomo (what's with the name again!), the Master has need of the room you have available. He told us to tell you that his appointed time had come but, first, he wanted to celebrate Passover with his disciples. Fine, I responded. That will be thirty shekels; you can have the space until 3:00 tomorrow afternoon and the room must be left exactly as you will find it. Agreed? Dear Sir, they said, we have no money. Jesus just told us that you would have a room available for him and his followers. You do have space available, don't you? I felt anger towards these men. Who does this Jesus think he is, I screamed at them? Do I look like some kind of charity? Remaining calm, one of the men said to me, I am sure Jesus will greatly reward you for your generosity to him and his friends. My mind went blank and my negotiating skills vanished. This was the last space available. I am tired of doing business today. I will just *give the room* to these people and make them go away. Go ahead, I blurted, you may occupy the room but be out by tomorrow afternoon and I will hunt you down if there is one thing broken or out of place. Now, go, and leave me alone. Tell your friend Jesus that he caught me in a weak moment but never ask me for a favor again! One of the men said to me, thank you, Schlomo. You are a generous man. Jesus will surely bless your kindness to him and his friends.

    I was furious with the men and myself. Had I gotten soft? How could I be so stupid to walk away from a handsome profit just because of some non-descript preacher from the country? Over a glass of wine at lunch, I had to admit that Jesus had gotten into my head. Perhaps he was right; with all my wealth, I could probably afford to share a little of my treasure with other less fortunate. I must grudgingly admit he has forced me to reflect on my life and how I am living it.

Schlomo felt his life was well ordered. His priorities made perfect sense to him. Then Jesus came along and nudged Schlomo off his comfortable track. Similar things have happened to us, haven't they? This story isn't about a money-grubbing miser who lived only for today. It is about any person who likes the status quo and believes that change may be threatening. Most of us don't like to step out of our groove; we might be required to do something that is scary or demands that we take action we don't like or want. Examples might include agreeing to take the chair of a civic committee, housing a foreign student for a term of study or teaching inner city school children to read. These things are inconvenient, hard work, impact your time and treasure and are not a lot of fun. But, each of us is called to share ourselves and our resources with others. What have you done lately to meet that requirement? Has your personal status quo become a little too comfortable? Think about what you might do to change that.

BARABBAS, THE CRIMINAL
Mt. 27: 15-22, 26

My father was the original rebel in our family. As a boy I clearly remember him railing against the Roman occupation of our country. He was always stirring up the people in our village with his vitriolic speeches condemning the unjust way we Jews were being treated by the Roman governors and soldiers. Sometimes he went beyond mere speeches. Often he would take overt action against the Romans. Some even went so far as to call it sabotage. Father would intentionally damage the buildings used by the soldiers as barracks. He would set fire to provisions, break the spokes on wagon wheels and take other actions that seriously aggravated the occupiers. He spent many a night in jail and was on the wrong end of countless Roman whips and similar punishments. Frankly, I was surprised that he did not wind up dead; I think the Romans kept him alive as an example to the rest of the people in the region. When he came home from a night or two in the local jail, he was usually a bloody mess from the beatings. This did not stop him. He continued to speak out for freedom and justice for the Jewish people.

I inherited my father's passion and stood by his side until the end of his life. I took up his mantle as the leader of the rebellious Jews and carried on my father's job of rousing the people and infuriating the illegal rulers of our country. My actions earned me the name Barabbas, which means son of the father. My real first name is Yeshua but few people called me that. Like my father before me, I spent many nights in the vile, stinking jail and spilled a lot of my blood on the filthy floor after beatings from the Roman guards. I will be honest—I hated those people from Rome with their superior attitude who looked down upon us Jews as second-class people not deserving of freedom.

Finally, my luck ran out. One evening, I was leading an organizing meeting of many like-minded Jews. A squad of soldiers burst into our meeting room and began arresting those in attendance. I fought back against the soldier assigned to detain me. We had a terrific struggle until I was able to wrest the dagger from his belt and used the knife to seriously wound him. To the other soldiers, I had done the unforgiveable—gravely injuring one of their own. Several of them overwhelmed me, shackled me and roughly dragged me off to the prison. I did not expect to survive the night.

In a large holding cell with me were many other prisoners. There was a lot of talk about some prophet named Jesus who was attracting a huge following. He was teaching the people with authority, healing the sick and performing all kinds of miracles. Some even said that Jesus was the long awaited Messiah, the one who would purportedly lead the Jews out of Roman bondage. Most amazing of all, Jesus proclaimed he was the son of the Father God. I listened to all this gossip with skepticism. He was the Messiah? Where was his army? He was the son of the Father? What a claim for a mere man to make! I was also amused by the startling similarity of our names. He was Jesus, son of the Father God. I was Yeshua, son of the father. In Aramaic, Jesus and Yeshua were almost identical, too. I told my jeering cellmates that this Jesus had stolen my name and I planned to tell him so if I ever had the chance to meet him in person.

Before dawn, I was dragged out of the cell and delivered to several soldiers who took great pleasure in beating me senseless with whips and sticks. As morning light appeared, I was hauled off to the local Roman commander. He listened briefly to testimony given by some of the soldiers who were present the prior evening. He quickly tired of their account and motioned them to be silent. Looking at me he said, you deserve death for your crimes. I am sending you to Pilate, the Procurator, who has the final say in such matters. But do not take heart, Jew, for Pilate will certainly confirm my judgment. To the soldiers he said, take this animal to Jerusalem.

While I am a brave man, I knew my life would come to an end before Passover was completed. Few welcome death but I had no regrets for the life I had lived. I felt acceptance for my fate but did not relish the long and exceedingly painful journey to the grave that the Romans were sure to arrange for me. There was riotous activity taking place as I was led into Pilate's palace courtyard. Soldiers at the ready were everywhere, and the open yard was filled with scribes and other members of the Jewish ruling class gesturing and calling to Pilate who sat on a stone bench elevated above the masses. As I was hauled up the steps towards Pilate, I caught sight of a man dressed in a purple robe, wearing a crown of woven thorns and obviously exhausted from a night of torture and beatings. As I reached a spot about ten feet from Pilate, the other prisoner looked steadily at me with a penetrating gaze. I felt he was looking directly into my soul. I heard one of my guards whisper to another soldier, that man is Jesus, the one all are talking about. So this is Jesus I thought. He doesn't look like a Messiah but he had an aura about him that raised the hair on my arms. The commander of my guard approached Pilate with a folded piece of paper, which he quickly read and then glanced at me. Pilate hushed the crowd and said to them, you have a tradition at your Passover that a prisoner is released to you. Which of these two men do you want me to release, this murderous thug Barabbas or Jesus? The crowd went into a frenzy and cried out, release Barabbas and crucify Jesus! Pilate weakly tried to argue but was drowned out. Stepping over to a basin of water, Pilate washed his hands, a ritual which meant he took no responsibility for this unjust decision. An aide to Pilate approached my guards and ordered them to remove me from the palace and then release me. It was unbelievable! I was to be set free but Jesus was to die. I couldn't explain my conflict and uneasiness with this decision. Why me and not him?

I never got over this brief encounter with Jesus. While we never spoke a word to one another, I felt closeness to him that I had never felt for another person. Was he the expected Messiah? Was he truly the son of the Father God? Was he human? Was he divine? Several days later I heard that he had arisen from the dead. Could this story be true? I plan to spend the rest of my life trying to find answers to these perplexing questions. The man with whom I shared a name was resurrected.

We often hear "life isn't fair." That is true. Two people with similar talents wind up having much different outcomes in their lives. Governments try to legislate solutions to this unfairness by attempting to create similar outcomes for all. These well-intentioned actions often exacerbate the problem but that is another story. Daily life is full of injustice for some people; many of us get the chance to witness this for ourselves. Equal work does not always fetch equal pay. Two students in the same town are offered vastly different educational choices. Some people are rich. Others are poor. Some succeed, some fail. Much injustice is not easily rectified. What do you do when you see injustice happening? Do you protest the unfairness of the situation? Do you take action to correct the unfairness? Do you feel any personal responsibility for injustice in the world? If not, how do you think your indifference may be judged? In this story, even Barabbas sensed that injustice was being committed against this stranger Jesus. Barabbas, who had followed his father fighting against injustice to his fellow Jews, sensed that Jesus was being treated unfairly. What would you have done in a similar situation?

ANTONIAS, CAPTAIN OF THE GUARD
Mt. 27: 54

I was born in the coastal city of Anzio, about eighty kilometers southwest from Rome. My family had a history of service in the Roman armies. Both my grandfather and father had served with distinction. It was expected that I would seek the same career when my time came. Grandfather and father told thrilling tales about their exploits, where they served, the victories won and the glorious triumphs. Even in retirement, they relished the camaraderie and the sense of brotherhood shared by their fellow soldiers. While they discussed the moments of ribaldry and exultation, they never talked about the violent deaths they witnessed, the horrible battle scars or their own personal wounds. Both of my forefathers carried several garish scars on their bodies as a result of military battles. Their remembrance of service always focused on the glory and never on the horror. It was probably just as well. I sat at their feet in rapt attention as they spun their yarns about the military. My imagination soared as I pictured myself leading a phalanx of soldiers into glorious, triumphant hand-to-hand combat with the enemy.

My father had been an officer, a Centurion in charge of one hundred soldiers. When I became seventeen, father was able to arrange for me to go to a special military training school that would prepare me to be both a soldier and an officer. The course was long and rigorous; several young men who had entered with me dropped out because of their inability to handle the taxing physical requirements or the demanding leadership training. I was enthusiastic about this new direction for my life and worked diligently to achieve success. Finally, I completed all the requirements and was assigned as a junior aide to a veteran Centurion named Caius. He was stern and demanding; I also observed that he treated his men fairly and justly especially when discipline or punishment was involved. He had chiseled good looks and a sense of leadership exuded from him. My responsibilities were as a junior officer. I found myself carrying messages from Caius to other commanders, arranging meetings for him with his subordinates and assuring that needed supplies for our unit were ordered. The best part of this assignment was being included in most of his meetings with both subordinates and superiors. While I was a mere fly on the wall during these sessions, I was absorbing some of the technical requirements of being an officer. I also saw how a veteran handled the personal rivalries, political posturing and infighting that inevitably exist in any large military organization. To me, a boy of eighteen, Caius seemed much older and mature than his twenty-six years would indicate. After some of these meetings, he would briefly take me aside and point out strategies he had employed or how he dealt with certain situations that had come up during the session. In spite of this personal tutoring, he studiously avoided familiarity. My association with Caius was strictly military and professional. He was my commander; I was expected to obey his orders quickly and loyally. His job was to prepare me for future expanded duties. That was the extent of our relationship.

Caius must have given his superiors favorable reports about my performance. After about one year, I was called in and told I was to be transferred to another unit, this time as the assistant commander (Tribune) to a Centurion leader. I considered this a handsome promotion and was very pleased, as was my father. Caius merely shook my hand and wished me good luck in my new assignment. My new leader was Centurion Pietras who represented a dramatic change from Caius. Pietras was a coarse, rude bully who treated his men badly, lived a libertine lifestyle and lead by fear and intimidation. He delegated many duties to me and offered little counsel or advice but was quick to scream his displeasure when things were not to his liking. I was growing up very quickly as a young Roman officer. Unfortunately, the common soldiers looked at me as a junior Pietras. Even though I employed the positive leadership skills taught to me by Caius, I was met with sullen disrespect by the men. This was obviously going to be a very difficult assignment. I longed for the opportunity to seek advice from Caius but that was not possible. Within a month or two, our unit was given orders to pack up and move to Jerusalem in Israel. I had heard much about this place; a godforsaken outpost full of unrest, bad living conditions and a populace that hated all Roman imperialists. Pietras showed his displeasure with this order and splashed his anger on all subordinates, including me. Packing all our material and supplies for the long trip by boat was a monumental job, all of which fell on me to organize. When we were finally underway headed east on Mare Nostrum, I was exhausted. The eight days at sea refreshed me physically but I sensed ominous signs about the future for my unit. Landing in the port city of Joppa, we immediately began the long march to our barracks located outside the walls of Jerusalem. Our quarters were ramshackle and dirty; the grumbling men were not pleased with my orders to repair and clean the facilities. In spite of obstacles, things began to take shape. Although they would never admit it, the refurbished barracks improved the morale of the men...but not Pietras, who was as surly as ever. How long must I endure this situation, I wondered?

All I had heard about this place was accurate. The climate was hot, dry and dusty; food was scarce and unappetizing; the populace was restive and hostile. Our assignment was to patrol and maintain order in one sector of Jerusalem close to the Procurator's palace where the principal Roman official, Pontius Pilate, lived. Even in difficult times, routine takes over. The unit quickly settled into a rhythm and I felt the men slowly reacting positively to my leadership. Pietras was often absent—I knew not where—so I was, *de facto*, the commanding officer. While general conditions were miserable, I began enjoying my command role and was gaining confidence in my ability to deal with most of the unplanned situations we faced. My sources were correct: the Jews were boiling beneath the surface. They chafed under Roman rule and I wondered when something big would happen. But day followed day and we only experienced a few tough incidents. I did observe one distressing character of almost all Roman soldiers: They were viciously brutal when dealing with Jewish citizens. I knew it was our job to maintain order but felt that the relentless and savage attitude of the soldiers was unnecessary in most cases. I wondered, would our unfeeling churlishness come back to haunt us one day? I admit I was uncomfortable with how we treated people generally.

One day, a subordinate delivered a letter to me. It was the first real letter I had ever received in my life! When I turned the packet over and saw the wax seal on the back, I could not believe my eyes. It was from Centurion Caius! I had not known that his unit had also been sent to Israel but was assigned in Galilee to the north. Caius got directly to the point. I am writing you, Antonias, because I was involved in an extraordinary event with a Jewish prophet named Jesus in this region. It was common knowledge that this Jesus was going throughout the area curing many sick people. While I do not subscribe to any religious teaching, I sought out Jesus because my personal slave was gravely ill, to the point of death. I thought, perhaps Jesus does have some magical powers to cure illness. It was worth a try. I approached him and told him about my chief servant's illness. Jesus was very kind to me, not defensive at all, and after hearing my plea told me that my servant would be healed. Soon after that brief encounter, one of my aides arrived and told me my slave had suddenly returned to complete health. No one at my household had any idea how this had happened because there was no treatment or medicines that had been given. I can only think that Jesus was behind this cure. I was so affected by this, Antonias, that I wanted to let you know in case you ever have the opportunity to see or hear this Jesus in your sector. I hope all is going well for you, young friend. Perhaps our paths will cross again in the future. (Signed) Caius.

I was thrilled to receive the letter and intrigued by what Caius had written. My mentor was not an emotional man; his encounter with Jesus must have profoundly touched him. I tucked the letter into my personal satchel, planning to read it again.

About two weeks later, at the beginning of the Passover festival week of the Jews, my unit was given an additional security assignment. The military leaders were worried about the possibility of civil unrest. We were assigned to patrol and protect an area called Golgotha, immediately outside the city gates. This site was frequently used to crucify brigands and criminals. I had heard a rumor that Jesus, whom Caius had spoken about, had arrived in Jerusalem to much fanfare. He had apparently caused a great deal of angst among the Jewish leaders and was being closely monitored by the Roman forces as well. I could feel the tension in the city and wondered where this might lead. On Friday, Pietras ordered me to take a contingent of troops to Golgotha to insure order was maintained. Heading to our assignment, we could hear the tumult near Pilate's palace, but I could not determine what was causing the commotion. My unit reached our assigned area shortly before noon. Within minutes, we saw a sea of people approaching our area. In the middle of the seething throng were three men carrying cross beams used for crucifixion. As they reached us, Roman soldiers from another unit were roughly manhandling the three men while preparing them for crucifixion. Their agonized cries could be heard above the din as each man suffered the ghastly pain of having his hands and feet nailed to the wooden planks on which they were hung. No amount of military training can prepare one to witness such brutality to another human being. Finally, each of the men was raised to an upright position as the crucifixion was completed. I learned from one of my comrades that the man in the middle was Jesus, the prophet Caius had written about. I went to the foot of his cross and looked up at him. His body had been ripped by a vicious flogging. On his head was a crown made of sharp thorns. Gasping for breath, he looked down upon me with an amazingly gentle gaze. I said to Jesus, Caius, the Centurion, told me that you cured his personal slave from a grave illness. Is that true? Looking intently at me, Jesus said, yes I did cure his servant. Caius is a man of integrity and honor. Would you also like me to do something for you, Jesus asked? Startled by this comment, I didn't immediately know how to respond. Finally, I said to Jesus, why don't you use your apparent power to save yourself from this brutal death on the cross? Managing a faint smile, Jesus said, no, I am fulfilling my Father's will. I had no idea what he meant. My father would never will me to suffer such anguish. What kind of a cruel father did Jesus have, I wondered?

Crucifixion is meant to be a slow, tortuous process. Jesus was cruelly tormented as planned. Since my soldiers and I were near the foot of his cross, we could hear him whenever he spoke or had conversation with his followers or the men crucified with him. Although he was in obvious distress, he seemed stoic and spoke without rancor. I heard him speak to the two other men crucified with him. He also spoke to his followers and family gathered near the foot of the cross. Several times he seemed to cry out to the wind with statements about abandonment and forgiveness. On multiple occasions I went back to stand below him. I asked him, is one of these nearby men your father? Why did your father require you to suffer such cruel treatment? Again, I was greeted with a gentle smile and gaze. Jesus said, my father is not of this world. He sent me so that I could redeem the people and open the gates of heaven to all believers. Do you believe in God? Jesus asked. I was now on unfamiliar ground. There had never been much talk in our home about religion. I knew little about the pantheon of Roman gods; they didn't affect my life one way or the other. What god are you talking about, I said to Jesus? His voice grew soft as he said, the Almighty God, my father in heaven with whom I am one in being along with the Spirit. Hearing these words both frightened and exalted me. Who is this man I am peering at? After a pause, I blurted out, well, it is over and done with but I am sorry that we were required to hang you on a tree like this. With the sweetest words I ever heard, Jesus said to me, I forgive you for what your soldiers have done to me. They...and you...have no idea who I really am. Hearing this sent a sudden shiver through my entire body. How can this man possibly forgive those of us who have treated him without the slightest shred of mercy?

The hours had passed slowly but it was now about 3:00 in the afternoon. During the last hour, the bright, sunny day had turned ominously dark as thick, black clouds swirled in the sky. Suddenly, there was a severe jolt...an earthquake! Just at that moment, I heard Jesus cry out, it is finished. With that, his head slumped and he apparently died. I was deeply touched. Turning to one of my soldiers, I said, surely this man was the Son of God. I have no idea what prompted me to say those words; they just came out of my mouth.

I will never forget the impression that Jesus made on me. From that moment on, my outlook on life and what is important was transformed. Within months I had a complete change of heart about a career in the military. I was disgusted with the inhumanity of our soldiers. The brief encounter with Jesus on a Friday afternoon profoundly altered me. My heart was now leading me to a life of service to my fellow man. Where this will ultimately lead, I do not yet know. But I do know that my soul is more at peace and I am convinced there is a purpose to my life that I had never before seen. I plan to let Caius know what has happened to me. Perhaps I will even seek out the small band of people who are spreading the word about Jesus. They may lead me to the next phase of my life.

Even to those of us who profess to be committed Christians, many go through the motions of a spiritual life, compartmentalized in one hour on Sunday morning at church with some brief prayer time in between weekly worship with a community. This is not a criticism; many lead too-busy lives that distract from deeper meditation or prayer. It is also correct that few of us are blessed with a true conversion experience. In our story, Antonias was blessed by a vivid epiphany when he personally encountered Jesus. Many of us are not so lucky. Ask God to send you a circumstance that deeply changes your life or your relationship with Him. It might be initially painful to actually alter directions but, in the long term, you may experience a glorious change in your life that includes a beautiful new understanding of the presence of God in your life.

BENJAMIN, THE PARALYTIC
Mk 2: 4-12

As a boy, my father let me work along side of him as he earned his living. My Abba formed and fired clay-roofing tiles used on homes and other buildings. He then would sell these tiles in the neighboring villages. Sometimes he bartered the tiles for household necessities our family needed. He showed me how to mix the clay and other ingredients, form the tiles and then fire them in the oven. Once in awhile, someone would ask my father to install the roof on a house. Most people could not afford this but some could, and there were others who had little ability when it came to constructing buildings. I really enjoyed helping Abba with his work, especially when I got the chance to assist him in building a roof.

After my father died, I continued the business. Because of my excellent training, I earned a reputation in the region for high quality tiles and could be relied upon to install a weather-tight and long lasting roof. Business was so good I actually began hiring men to help me. I must admit that I wasn't easy to work for. While my father had been very patient with me as I learned, I demanded perfection from my employees and accepted no excuses for poor workmanship. I think the men were so happy to have employment that they put up with my harsh treatment. I felt guilty sometimes because each of the four men I eventually hired were all good men who worked very hard and were good at their jobs.

My life forever changed one fateful day. We had been hired to install a roof on a new home being constructed by the community's richest man, a cloth merchant. My helpers and I were placing the cap tiles on the ridge of the roof. Suddenly, I slipped and fell off the roof. I had fallen about fifteen feet and landed on my back where there was a rocky patch of ground. I knew immediately that I had been seriously injured. My colleagues rushed to help me, but I could see in their faces that I was in grievous trouble. In addition to pain, I had numbness and tingling in my hands and feet. Soon it became apparent that I could not move my arms and legs. My life flashed before me: what would I do? How would I support my family? Would I become a dependent cripple relying on the charity and kindness of others? I was terrified that life, as I knew it, was over for me.

It took several weeks to confirm my worst fears. The workers continued to operate the business, but they did not have the experience or necessary skills so activity was steadily dwindling. I was almost totally paralyzed, a helpless wretch humiliated by my reliance on others for the most basic of human care. I cursed God for allowing this to happen to me. We Jews believed that bad things never happen to good people. What had I possibly done to deserve this cruel and hateful situation to descend upon me? I quickly became a bitter and unlovable person.

Around our village there was a lot of talk about Jesus who many called a prophet and some even the Messiah. People told the most amazing stories about Jesus, especially the healing that he did. Excitement peaked when we heard that Jesus was coming to our little community. Even though I was very skeptical about these so-called miracle workers, I did ask my employees if they would take me to the place where Jesus was to speak. I am ashamed to say my bad temper continued even as they carried my stretcher to the meeting place. I could not stop yelling at these four men to be careful. Don't drop me. Watch where you are going. I was certainly an ungrateful and sour person. Secretly, I was surprised that they even agreed to take me to see Jesus.

When we arrived at the scene, there was a massive crowd of people all wishing to see and hear Jesus.

Obviously, we had arrived too late since the site of the meeting was already full to overflowing. No one else could possibly get inside. I was disappointed but resigned. I rationalized that seeing Jesus would have done me no good anyway so why should I be bothered. I noticed my four employees conferring together. They came to me and said they were going to lift me up to the roof, remove some of the tiles and lower me down into the room where Jesus was. Their faith was much greater than mine; they were convinced Jesus could cure my infirmity. They did as promised, hoisting me to the roof, creating a hole and lowering my stretcher mat into the room. Looking up to see me descending from the ceiling, Jesus looked slightly amused. I felt somewhat awkward, but Jesus had a warm smile and seemed to be genuinely interested in me as I reached the floor in front of him. He asked me who had helped me on the roof. He also was interested in why I felt it was important to meet him this way. My answer was probably rambling, but he listened intently with a smile on his face. Finally, as I lay there Jesus said to me, Benjamin, your sins are forgiven. I immediately remembered how unfair and unkind I had been to my employees. Jesus' words lifted these unjust actions from my shoulders and I felt cleansed and unburdened from my petty behavior toward these wonderful men who were trying to help me. After that, I heard angry words directed at Jesus. A temple official asked him by what authority he forgave sins. Only God can forgive sins, the official said. Jesus responded by asking which was easier: to forgive sins or to cure the person? To make his point, Jesus looked at me intently and said, rise, pick up your mat and go home. I immediately felt as if I had been immersed in clear, warm water. My pain was gone! I saw that I could move my arms and legs. I was stunned by what was happening! First, I sat up then lifted myself up from the stretcher and stood in front of Jesus. I was cured! How did this happen? I looked at Jesus and tried to stammer my thanks but found myself speechless. While this was occurring, the house full of people had been quiet. When they saw me get up, the room erupted in noise. I heard words praising God, excited sounds and cries of fear for what they had just witnessed. I walked, ...yes, walked...through the throng and left the house. I was greeted there by my four friends who hugged me and gently patted me on the back. Washing over me was a sense of gratitude. This thanks started with Jesus, of course, but more importantly to these wonderful four men that I had never fully appreciated. In spite of my verbal lashes and unfair treatment, they stayed loyal...and loving...to me. Because of their determination, I had a brief encounter with Jesus. He cured my physical body for which I am eternally grateful. But curing my soul may have been the more important thing he did for me that evening.

All of us have family, friends, neighbors or co-workers that we interact with every day. Because God is invisible to our human eyes, we are told we will find the face of God in the people we encounter in our daily lives. How often we take these folks for granted. Worse yet, we find we don't even like some of these people. It is important for each of us to figure out how to do God's will during the few earthly days we have to live. We also need to learn what God will require of us when we make an accounting to him, face-to-face, at the end of our time on this earth. Actually, God has been pretty clear about what he is looking for. Check out the Gospel of Matthew, Chapter 25, Verses 31-46. All scripture has been written to help us on our salvation journey. But these passages from Matthew provide a specific roadmap for our journey through the veil of human life into eternal life. These ideas must be etched on our souls.

LEGION, THE POSSESSED MAN
Mk. 5: 2-20

    I was a terrible, wretched human being. While many so-called doctors had examined me, not one of them could tell me what was wrong or what could be done to cure me of my crazy, erratic and bizarre anti-social behavior. I also possessed enormous strength so most of the people in the nearby towns were terrified when they saw me. I hated my life and things seemed to get worse every day. I was totally alone, afraid, isolated from human contact and living a horrible existence with awful food, rags for clothes and a dirty, leaking hovel for shelter. I had learned that there are many things worse than death and that included the life I was leading.

    It all started when I was young boy. I was not like the other kids in my village. I couldn't play without getting into fights with playmates. Often I would shout and curse others for no apparent reason. My parents tried hard to raise me, but I never seemed to cooperate with them. My actions finally became so disruptive to our family life that one day my father came to me with great tears in his eyes and said, Son, we are deeply sorry but you can no longer stay as a member of our family. Your refusal, or inability, to become a part of our little group of people is distressing your mother and me and your siblings; therefore, you cannot live with us any longer. I am desperately sorry to say these words to you but I have no other choice. We have put some food and extra clothes into a sack for you but now you must leave and find another place to live. Where that will be, I do not know. We will continue to love you, son, but you must leave. We ask that the gods care for you.

First, I felt overwhelming rage. My flesh burned as I heard these words from my father. I thought about killing him on the spot; with my size, I could have easily strangled him to death. Then I felt absolute desolation and fear. Where would I possibly go? How would I feed myself after the few scraps provided by my father were gone? What am I to do? Is my life over? Perhaps this would have been a blessing.

I wandered away aimlessly from my village. People crossed to the other side of the path and averted their eyes as I approached them on the road. Yes, I knew that something was wrong with me; there was no denying that fact. But, what had I done to deserve such complete ostracism? Upon reaching a lonely stretch of road, I sat down on a nearby rock and burst into a long, sobbing wail that lasted for an extended time until my tears were used up. I would have gladly welcomed a bolt of lightning or the tip of a Roman spear through my heart to end this misery that was consigned to me.

Looking up, I saw a figure approaching me on the road. He was a tall and well dressed man who showed no sign of fear as he drew closer. Reaching me he stopped and began a conversation. You look very distressed, he said; what is going on with you? Even though he was a total stranger, I blurted out what had happened to me and how desperate I was especially with the thought of being totally alone. A small smile curled over his lips. I think I can be of help to you, he said. I happen to control the spirits of many who are looking for some person to live with. They would be good company for you and you would never be alone again. I have the power to bring these spirits to reside within you. Would you like to have them join you? That way, I can promise you that you will always have companions for the rest of your life. Say yes and your current problem of isolation will be over.

This man's talk was so alluring and filled with promise. I wanted to say yes but I didn't understand how this could be done. Please, sir, tell me how this can be accomplished? The man again smiled and with a soft voice said, just trust me and say yes and your troubles will end. My head said no but my heart said yes. I turned to the man and said yes, as he had wished. He let out a deep guttural laugh and patted me firmly on my back. It is done, then, he said. Sir, what is your name? How shall I call you? You may call me Lucifer, he purred. You shall see me again. He quickly departed, heading in the direction I had come from.

Immediately I began to hear voices in my head. There were hundreds, perhaps thousands of them. They were screeching, screaming and wailing words that made no sense. They cursed God, their fate, all the earth, and me. Nothing I did would stop this terrible noise. Lucifer had tricked me with his cool blandishments. Companions? No, merely more demons to inhabit my soul. Now things were more horrible than before if that were possible. I wanted to die. My new companions were driving me insane.

I took refuge in a nearby graveyard. In my frenzy, I desecrated the tombs, tore limbs off trees and cursed God day and night. Local town officials came out to subdue me and chain me to the trees, but I would always break free after they had left. The demons warned me about a Jew named Jesus. The voices told me to avoid any contact with this man since he was certain to visit even more trouble on me. Because the local area was populated with mostly pagans and Gentiles it was unlikely Jesus would visit the region but, if he did, stay away from him, the voices shrieked.

One day, I saw a large group of people walking on the road that passed the tombs. My voices yelled at me, stay away! Jesus is in that group. Ignoring my demons, I ran to the road and prostrated myself before Jesus. He said to me, unclean spirits, come out of this man! I replied to Jesus, what are you doing to me, Jesus, the

Son of God? Please leave me alone and don't torment me further. What is your name, he asked me? I replied that my name was Legion because I was full of demons. There was a nearby herd of swine. Through my voice, the demons pleaded with Jesus to send them into the pigs. With that, Jesus forced the demons out of me and into the swine. There was a nearby steep bank that led down to the sea. When the demons entered the swine, the pigs rushed frantically down the embankment into the water and drowned. Those men tending the pigs were deeply afraid and ran into the nearby town to report these events.

    Meanwhile, Jesus and I had been speaking to one another. I had never felt so calm and happy in my entire life. I heard no voices. I felt no compulsion to scream, shout and curse God. I actually felt like a normal person. Who was this miracle worker who made me feel so at peace? He continued to speak to me with reassuring words about my life and what my future would be like. Whoever this man was, I owed my life and sanity to what he had done for me.

    Hearing the stories of the swineherds, the town people came out to see Jesus. They were frozen with fear about what had happened. Because they had no understanding of God, they didn't know what to think. But they pleaded with Jesus to leave their region. He had thoroughly upset and confused them and they wanted him gone at once. With a certain sadness, Jesus agreed to leave and proceeded to the shore to enter a boat. I followed and begged him to let me remain with him as one of his followers. No, Jesus said, I want you to go home and tell your family what has happened to you and let them know that you are now well because of what the Lord in his love has done for you.

    A man named Jesus saved my life, I told my family and neighbors. My new life was now full of love, peace, productivity, happiness and normal relationships with the people I encountered. Thank you, Jesus, for what you have done for me.

Have you ever felt totally alone or disconnected from the people around you? What about the first day in a new school? Attending a large meeting where you didn't know a single soul? Moving to a new city with no friends or family nearby? Beginning a new job in a very large company? Attending a church where no one greeted you, smiled or offered you a cup of coffee afterwards? Most of us have experienced some type of isolation in our lives. It is uncomfortable, often scary and frequently upsetting. Of all the problems faced by Legion in this story, isolation traumatized him the most. Jesus reached out and healed this deepest of all wounds. What is the message for us? Since we know how lonely separation from others can be, we must be on the alert for others who may be facing this kind of a problem. You and I can offer a kind word, a gentle smile, an offer of directions to find a needed resource or a simple hello, may I help you in any way? Those little things are what we are called to do. Small gestures can make a terrific difference.

DAN, THE MONEY CHANGER
Mk. 11: 15-19
Lk. 19: 45-46
Jn. 2: 13-16

I was raised in a conventional Jewish home. We lived in Emmaus, a village about seven miles from the Holy City, Jerusalem. Our parents kept a strictly Kosher home. We followed all the dietary laws carefully, observed feast days and attended temple services every week. I am not bragging about this; virtually all of our neighbors, friends and relatives followed the same religious program in their lives, too. We belonged to a sect called Pharisee. That meant we believed in the resurrection of all people at the end of the world and things like angels and spirits. All of these religious beliefs and practices were comfortable to our household and offered a spiritual pace to our daily lives. I loved my family, my relatives, friends and neighbors, my temple and my God. In return, I felt valued and was content with my life generally. Like any youngster growing up, I didn't think everything was fair but that is the nature of young people who have not yet reached full maturity.

My father performed the important function of a moneychanger in the temple. The coins used by the Roman occupiers could not be used in the great temple in Jerusalem to pay the tax or for the purchase of small birds and animals used in special sacrifices. Jews believed deeply that no graven image should enter God's house; money with Caesar's image on its face could not be used for a holy purpose so the moneychangers performed a valuable and pious service to worshippers. Those who served as spiritual bankers used a rate of exchange that allowed them to make a small profit on each transaction. At the end of a busy day in the temple, my father brought home a handful of coins that provided sustenance for our family. I believe he treated everyone fairly and would never gouge a distant visitor with an unjust rate of exchange. When my father died, I continued the practice of exchanging money in the temple. He had been a good teacher so I was well prepared for these duties. Like my father, I had a reputation of fairness.

Observant Jews all believed in the concept of a Messiah. Scripture was full of stories and information about the one who would eventually come to restore Israel and the Jewish people to their rightful place as God's chosen race and their homeland as a location of continuing grace and bounty. There was little agreement, however, on the exact timing of the Messiah's coming, how he would be recognized or what he would do to restore God's kingdom. Scripture was full of allegory, ambiguous passages and nuanced references to the Messiah, so there were lively arguments among the scholars and religious lawyers about exactly what all this meant. The majority of average folks believed the coming of the Messiah would be a clear and certain event that eliminated further disputes.

During my lifetime, a number of so-called prophets emerged as popular preachers. Some of them were even thought to be the Messiah sent from God and were happy to claim that title for themselves. Over time—sometimes long, sometimes short—all of these "Messiahs" disappeared into the fog of history. Some had a message that did not hold together, others lost the peoples' attention and some turned out to be full of human faults and vices. Most people said, don't get too excited when you hear the Messiah has arrived. We think it will be pretty obvious when it actually happens. At least, that is what my father taught us.

The role of the money changers in the temple was undergoing a serious and unfortunate change. Because the service offered a chance to make money, competition increased. Instead of a handful of exchange locations, the temple seemed to be swarming with people offering the "best deal" to visitors. Those doing the exchange also began to increase the services they offered. In addition to swapping money, the pseudo-bankers were also selling turtle doves and animals used in sacrifices. The area of the temple occupied by these activities was turning into a frantic bazaar, filled with shouts about money and things for sale. What had been a dignified religious utility was becoming a tawdry display of greed that sullied the spiritual visitor to the temple. A job I once loved and was proud to do was becoming very distasteful to me. How I wished I could return to being a humble servant to the temple guests, assisting them in their quest for a spiritual experience in this magnificent building constructed for worshipping God.

Visitors to the temple could not escape hearing about the new prophet, Jesus. He was raised in Nazareth but now lived in Capernaum. Temple tourists spoke with awe and wonder about his powerful teaching and the amazing cures and miracles he was supposedly doing. Like many others hearing these stories for the first time, I shrugged and said, I'll wait to see what happens. Was this to be just another short-lived Messiah adventure? Probably, so I wasn't getting my hopes up. But every day the stories persisted and glowing reports were provided by very credible people. I wondered, could this really be the one? Well, I would like to see him and hear him speak, I thought, but it will probably turn out to be nothing.

On the Sunday before Passover, there was quite a stir around the temple. This Jesus was in Jerusalem and many people were greeting his visit with great enthusiasm. It was said he planned to visit the temple during his stay. Perhaps I would get my chance to see him and hear him speak. Mid-week, while I was about my duties, I heard a great commotion a short distance from my exchange booth. People were shouting and darting about as a man walked down the row of moneychangers tipping over tables and opening cages to let turtledoves escape. Men were frantically trying to pick up the money that had been splayed across the temple floor. Relentlessly, the man continued down the line upsetting tables and chairs. I heard him exclaim, you have made my father's house a den of thieves. I turned to the man in the booth next to mine and asked, who is this man causing all this upset? He excitedly responded, this is Jesus the prophet about whom you have heard. I have no idea what he is doing. In his wake, Jesus had left the moneychangers in disarray. He finally reached my booth but did not turn over my table as he had done with others. Instead, he looked at me and said, Dan, you have provided fair treatment to temple visitors. Continue to offer just service and you will be blessed. He smiled, briefly gripped my hand and headed towards the exit of the temple followed by arm-waving angry bankers and merchants and a handful of his followers.

    I stood near my table in stunned silence. This was not the encounter with Jesus that I had expected. The money changing area looked like it had been hit by lightning. Tipped over and broken tables and chairs, open bird cages and coins scattered around the stone floor. The few words Jesus spoke to me were so kind and full of hope. Even though I had not said one word in response, I felt as if I had an extended conversation with the man. I experienced peace and the glow of joy in my soul after Jesus departed. Somehow, I felt changed, renewed and reinvigorated by the brief encounter. Returning home that evening I thought seriously about my role—however slight—in making the temple a special and holy place for visitors. Yes, I vowed, I will treat people as Jesus directed me to do.

    Generosity. What is it? We often think of generosity in terms of wealth and how it is shared by those who have it with those who do not. We hear of the rich uncle who helps his numerous nieces and nephews with money for college tuition. Or, the indulgent father who always insures his own children have the latest electronic gadgets and a nice auto to drive. Universities and churches rely on the generosity of wealthy alumni or congregants to fund growth in programs or needed new facilities. Observe what happens when some section of the world is struck by a massive natural disaster. Generous people freely give funds to assuage the misery experienced by the affected populace. Most of us are pretty clear what generosity means in the context of money. Generosity extends to other things as well: time and talent. In today's frenetic world one of the commodities in shortest supply is personal time. All of us seem to be "on the go" at full speed throughout most days. Whether it is work or school, shuttling children to and fro, providing care to a relative or friend—every moment seems filled. To give time as a reading assistant or a teacher's aide in the classroom, fund raising for Little League or the Girl Scouts, volunteering in a prison ministry or chairing a committee at your church all require the generous gift of one's time. And, don't forget generosity with talent. Think about those who volunteer to teach computer basics to senior citizens, or those who use skills to help with Habitat for Humanity. Many doctors and nurses work in pro bono clinics using medical skill to help the indigent. Yes, generosity takes many forms: treasure, time and talent. In what ways have you been generous to others? Even if you cannot give money, are you willing and able to provide your time or talent to others? Dan, the moneychanger, was prepared to forego big profits to offer a rich spiritual environment to visitors to the temple in Jerusalem. If your generosity has been limited in the past—for whatever reason—can you see how it might be possible to share your treasure, time or talent?

JEHUDI, THE SCROLL ATTENDANT
Lk. 4: 16-22

I have always lived in Nazareth. Everyone had a difficult life there; the great majority of people worked hard to scratch out a basic existence. There is a pleasant side of living here, too. Most of the townspeople came from the same clan, so there were many degrees of cousins and other relatives close by. Folks got along pretty well, so when it came time for feasts, weddings, welcoming new children and other happy occasions, the celebrations became pretty lively and enthusiastic. I am fortunate; my mother and father are still alive and I live in my parent's home with my younger brother and two younger sisters. My father basically earns his living by processing olives he has grown in nearby orchards. His products are good to eat. He prepares them by covering the olives with a mix of herbs and then soaks them in oil. While there was not a lot of money in circulation, father has loyal customers who enjoy his products. His earnings produce a modest life for the family, but we were always taught to be very thankful for the many blessings God bestowed upon the six of us.

My parents faithfully attend our local temple. From age seven, I was sent weekly to the Yeshiva where I received instruction in the Torah. While many boys my age were reluctant students, I loved the classes. I was particularly fascinated with the beautiful scrolls that contained the sacred scripture writings. Our teachers impressed upon us the covenant between God and mankind that was so mystically described in the Torah. I worked diligently in Yeshiva and often earned the right to read from the scrolls as my Hebrew language skills increased. Scroll reading was a highlight of my week.

I remember one other boy who attended class with me. His name was Joshua or Yeshua; twenty-five years later I can't recall his name exactly. I mentioned that some of my fellow students were not enthusiastic about their studies but that was not true for this boy. It seemed that he had received some special tutoring. The studies for him were not the least bit challenging. He had no difficulty reading and he often posed questions for the Rabbi that displayed a deeper understanding of the scriptures than any of the rest of us possessed. I also remember that he was not a braggart or a show off because of his knowledge and skills. He was very friendly to all of us and would be willing to help us when we came across a new word or an especially difficult passage. I liked him a lot personally but, for some reason, our paths away from Yeshiva did not seem to cross very often. I do know that he was quite busy helping his father, a man named Joseph, in his carpentry business. We grew to manhood together and when we did run into each other, it was always a pleasant and cordial exchange. I wish I could remember his name!

I finally lost track of him. I was told that he had moved from Nazareth to Capernaum. Meanwhile I continued to be very active at the temple. The chief Rabbi had remembered what a good student I had been as a young man in Yeshiva. When there was an opening for a scroll attendant at the temple, the Rabbi asked me to assume this duty. I felt extremely honored to be appointed because I had never lost my awe of the scrolls that held the Torah. My new job required me to retrieve the scrolls from the beautifully carved cabinet where they were kept. The cabinet in our little temple was a miniature representation of the Ark of the Covenant. What a blessing it was for me to handle the Torah each week as we gathered for prayer.

After the temple service most of the people would linger awhile to catch up on the latest news and gossip.

There was increasing talk about a new Rabbi who was gaining a lot of attention from the people. Apparently, this man was a cousin and friend of John the Baptist who was quite well known in the area. This new preacher, we were told, originally came from Nazareth. When I heard his name—Jesus—I finally recalled the boy I had gone to school with. Ah, yes, Jesus was his name. How could I have forgotten? I remembered him well. He had seemed uniquely gifted at the time but I had no idea he might turn out to be a prominent itinerant preacher. I find it most intriguing to observe how many of our young men turned out as they reached maturity. I was eager to see Jesus again and hoped that his travels might sometime return him to his home city. It would be pleasant to re-acquaint, I thought, and hear the religious message he was delivering in the region.

Sure enough, one day we heard that Jesus planned a visit to Nazareth to see some relatives. Our Rabbi invited Jesus to speak in our temple. All the congregants were looking forward to hearing him. The day arrived and Jesus came to the temple with a small group of his disciples. I immediately went to him and shook his hand saying, do you remember me from Yeshiva? I am Jehudi. Jesus gave me a warm smile and said, of course I remember you, Jehudi. It is a great blessing to see you again. I was delighted that he could recall our student days. As the service began, I proudly presented the scroll to Jesus. It was open to a passage from Isaiah that foretold the coming of the Messiah. He read the scripture beautifully with a rich voice and using perfect pacing. When he concluded, there was utter silence in the room and everyone was looking at him intently. He slowly rolled up the scroll and handed it back to me. He had mesmerized everyone including me. After several moments, he looked around the room and began to speak again slowly so as to be clearly understood. Today this scripture passage is fulfilled in your hearing, Jesus proclaimed. Once more there was silence but now the people began looking at one another. Finally a whisper could be heard. Did you hear what I did, said one man? Soon a clamor of conversation could be heard. One man called out to Jesus saying, aren't you the son of the carpenter Joseph? Are you, a mere village man, claiming now to be the anointed one, the Messiah? Jesus looked intently at the questioner but said nothing. More angry voices were now heard. How dare you claim this title for yourself, one yelled. Remaining calm in the face of the agitated temple members Jesus said, I did not expect to be understood or accepted in my hometown. He pointed out that the prophet Elijah had faced the same rejection. Many in the temple took this criticism very personally and began fomenting the crowd to physically drive Jesus out of the temple. All the while, I was in shock over what was occurring. Many had left their seats and were gathering around Jesus angrily. They roughly grabbed him and began dragging him out of the building. I heard one hysterical voice say, let's take him to the hill outside the village and throw him off the cliff. This blasphemer deserves to die! There was a crush of people heading toward the hill. I followed behind feeling helpless and afraid for my old friend. As they reached the brow of the hill, the cluster of people who had been tightly holding Jesus separated slightly. He had disappeared from the very middle of the crowd! Where had he gone? The angry and furious mob could not believe he had escaped.

    I was left shaken and heartsick. Jesus had been so charismatic. His words in the temple had given me such hope even though I was perplexed by his claim to be the Messiah. Our meeting was too brief; I wanted to speak to him more and find out everything about the message he was taking to the people of Israel. The following week at temple was full of agitation and disruption. No one had recovered from the events of last week, including me. The entire service seemed strained and irreverent somehow. I decided that I must go and find Jesus and hear more of what he was saying. I felt sure the local religious community could never again nurture my spiritual longing for a closer relationship to God, one even I didn't understand until I saw Jesus again.

Have you ever thought about why you go to church and the blessing of the experience? It is a sad fact that many of us attend religious services because of cultural habit. Most people were influenced by their parents and led by the hand to visit church weekly. We continue attending church even now because, well, we have always gone to church on the weekend. We need to ask ourselves: is this church experience changing us? Does it reshape our values, bring us closer to our God, and provide us with incentive to love our neighbors more? Honestly, is weekly church attendance merely 1/168th of the total hours available to us during a week? It is often said that even people who are faithful, regular members of their congregations seldom undergo a genuine conversion experience. How about you? Has there been a time in your life when the light of grace exploded in your soul, changing everything for you? If not, do you think you would like to go through such a conversion? This sounds like an easy question...sure, I want to feel closeness to my God, to have a deeper spiritual awakening. But it is risky to seek such a dramatic change. What if God, enjoying this new intimacy with you, begins to ask you to do things you have never done before? What if he asks you to abandon old habits, quit being judgmental of others and begin loving people you haven't much cared for previously? Jehudi, the scroll attendant, was quite content with the mechanical and mundane things of his weekly temple gathering. Then, his soul was seared by the words of his former classmate, Jesus. Why don't you ask God to take you through the same kind of conversion experience Jehudi faced? Who knows? It could change your life forever.

SIMON, THE CYRENIAN
Mark 15: 21

    My home city, Cyrene, has an interesting history. Several hundred years ago, Ptolemy I, king of Egypt, took control of this city located on the north coast of Africa just west of Egypt's border. The city is adjacent to the Great Sea or Mare Nostrum as the Romans call it. Ptolemy I was an important friend of Alexander the Great and served as a trusted general to Alexander during many significant campaigns. Although in Africa, Cyrene has a very large Jewish population. That is because Ptolemy I forced most Jews out of Egypt during his reign and many of us—my ancestors—wound up here. Intermarriage during the past several hundred years has resulted in large numbers of us being black skinned people, as I am. I have a sense of pride in living in Cyrene. I am also proud of my Jewish heritage, my black skin and the fact that I am a hard working businessman with two wonderful sons, Rufus and Alexander. By the way, my younger son was named after Alexander the Great whose exploits I greatly admired.

    I have been a devout Jew all my life. I regretted that I never celebrated Passover in Jerusalem. Last year I finally decided I would travel to the Holy City this spring. In addition to observing Passover there, I would have a chance to visit my two sons who live in that area. My third reason for traveling was to possibly increase the reach of my business by contacting several prospective customers in Jerusalem. I was excited about this trip and set forth on a ship from the port at Cyrene. After several uneventful days at sea, I landed at the city of Joppa in Judea, not far distant from Jerusalem. Rufus, my son, met me there and together we headed to Jerusalem. It was great to see him again. While traveling, he brought me up to date on his life and what was happening in the region.

Rufus was enthusiastic about an itinerant preacher he had met named Jesus. Rufus told me that he and his brother, Alexander, were spending as much time as they could traveling around Galilee with Jesus to hear him preach, see him perform cures of the sick and do other amazing things. Speaking from a committed heart, Rufus told me he believed Jesus was a special prophet and might even be the Messiah we all awaited. I love and trust Rufus but recalled hearing one story after another about new prophets with Messiah complexes. They came and went with regularity. I said to Rufus, son, don't get overly fervent about this man Jesus. There have been many in the past that we thought might be the Messiah but they turned out to be like shooting stars in the night sky...explosive bursts of light that quickly faded away and turned to dust.

My son told me that Jesus had traveled from Galilee to Jerusalem this past week and was wildly greeted by adoring crowds. Rufus said that both the Romans and the Jewish leaders were very concerned about how excited people were with Jesus. The Jews didn't like him because he upset the status quo; the Romans didn't like him because he posed a threat to civil order and Roman rule. His growing popularity was not welcomed by either leadership faction. What will come of this no one knows, said Rufus. He continued, anyway, Father, you may have an opportunity to meet and hear Jesus during the time you are here.

My two sons had arranged for a couple of small rooms to use during the Jerusalem visit. The accommodations were spartan but I was so pleased to be with my boys that I really didn't care. Since this was my first visit to the Holy City, my sons gave me a tour. What a magnificent city it was! I thoroughly enjoyed seeing everything I could and stored pictures in my mind's eye so I could tell everyone when I got back home. Jesus was the main topic of conversation wherever we went. The stories I heard about what Jesus had done were quite incredible but Rufus and Alexander kept telling me that all I was hearing was true. Although we traveled throughout the city, we never did encounter Jesus; several times people said to us, you just missed him—he was here minutes ago. Passover arrived and we arranged to celebrate the ritual feast with a small group of visitors to the city. It was so uplifting for me to celebrate Passover in the Holy City with my two beloved sons. I felt very blessed indeed.

The following morning, the city was abuzz. Jesus had been arrested the prior evening and was now in the Procurator's palace facing some type of trial and punishment for his so-called crimes against civil order. My sons and I tried to get close to the scene hoping to obtain better information but the streets were chaotic and crowded. Around 11:00 in the morning, the boys left me in a market square and said they were going to look for some of Jesus' disciples who might have better facts about the situation. They told me to stay where I was and they would return as soon as possible. Suddenly, coming up the street was a throng of people headed by a group of soldiers roughly clearing the street of bystanders. Following the soldiers were hundreds of folks hugging the pathway next to the buildings on either side of the roadway. In the middle of the road was a bloodied, beaten man staggering along and carrying a very large piece of rough hewn timber. It was a scene out of hell. The soldiers were screaming orders and cursing everyone in their way. Those following the man were wailing or taunting him with every kind of vile epithet. I stood by the side of the road frozen by the experience. I had no idea what I should do. Just as the man reached a spot within five feet of me, he tripped and fell. The heavy piece of lumber landed on his back as he hit the hard stone pavement. Looking at him, I thought he might be dead; he did not move or make any sound while lying on the road. One of the soldiers in charge glanced around and spotted me. He grabbed my tunic and pulled me toward the man. You, black man, pick up that timber and carry it for this criminal. No, I said, I don't want to get involved. I know nothing about this man. The Roman snarled to me, do as I say or you'll get even worse than he's getting. The soldiers forced me to pick up the timber. It was enormously heavy and rough, full of splinters. The man was pulled to his feet and began again to lurch onward. I was next to him. He turned to me and looked at me with a glance I can only describe as thankful and loving. If I didn't know better, I would say that he knew me as a friend who had come to rescue him in a moment of distress. When I heard his name called from the crowd, I was stunned. This is Jesus? This is the man my boys idolize? He looks like just a poor, ravaged bloody mess of a man who is near to death. But that look in his eye; I can't get over how that made me feel. The soldiers were roughly treating me, forcing me to drag the timber. Jesus was next to me, gasping for breath. Occasionally, he would turn his head toward me and give a grateful smile, almost like a blessing. I finally had courage to say to him, Jesus, can you make it? He smiled and replied, yes, dear Simon, with your help, I will make it. How did he know my name? We traveled several hundred more paces before reaching a small knoll outside the gates of the city. There, the executioners waited. I dropped the timber and darted back into the crowd before the soldiers could further mistreat me. I wondered: why was I picked? Hundreds of his friends lined the roadway; yet they picked me to help him, a stranger, a foreigner, a black man. I admit...I was terribly shaken by the experience. And yet, I was drawn to Jesus. In his anguish, he showed me kindness, love and a gentle nature. I shall never forget those brief minutes when I walked side-by-side with Jesus on the way to his own crucifixion.

My two sons tracked me down soon after. I told them of my moving encounter with Jesus. My clothes were torn and my shoulders and hands bloody and full of splinters. Yet, I felt euphoria in my soul. Yes, my dear sons, I shall never forget this rendezvous with Jesus for the rest of my life. I have been forever changed. How or why or what it means I do not know. But, nothing will ever be the same in my life since I met Jesus face-to-face.

From a young age we were taught by our parents to avoid strangers. We are programmed in infancy that unfamiliar people may have dark intentions about us; therefore, shun them and do not trust them (with the possible exception, the child is reminded, of a police officer). As we grow to adulthood remnants of this training stick with us. We avoid eye contact on the sidewalk or bus. In crowds we are careful not to invade a stranger's space. These actions leave me and others isolated. Juxtaposed is Jesus' command to love our neighbor as ourselves. But the stranger we avoid and the neighbor we must love are the same, are they not? Although a stranger, Simon of Cyrene was selected to be the neighbor of Jesus, offering help when help was most needed. Who are the Simons in your life? Who walks beside you daily that might offer you aid if only you would ask? Is it a neighbor? A friend? A co-worker? Your spouse? We must all learn to find our own Simons, strangers only because we have not reached out to them with love. They are people who can help us, people to whom we extend our friendship and trust and even share our human fears, vulnerabilities and weakness. Can you identify your Simons? Are there others who may look upon you as their Simon? Strangers no more, but neighbors and friends sharing life's wonderful and desperate moments together.

HILIEL, THE PHARISEE TESTING JESUS
Matthew 22: 34-36

My earliest remembrance as a boy was my father frequently explaining to his children our family's association with the Pharisee sect. Father obviously felt it was important for us to understand what the Pharisees believed. He also explained how we differed from the Sadducees who represented the other major group in Israel's religious and political structure historically. He impressed upon my brothers and me that the Pharisees had come into existence about four hundred years before and that Esdras, sometimes called Ezra, was a leading founder and prophet in the movement, if you could call it that. Father would often quote from scripture, especially the books related to the Maccabee clan that seemed to chronicle the beginning of the Pharisees. Most importantly, we were taught to be devoted to Mosaic Law, as written in the sacred Torah but also to believe the oral traditions from Moses' time that were memorialized in the Talmud and Mishnah.

These instructions during my youth certainly formed my thinking as I reached the maturity of an adult man. Now I have my own family and I continue the tradition of passing on the heritage and belief system that had been given to me. More than that, I studied the Torah and Talmud in great depth. While modesty forbids me from saying so, many of my friends and acquaintances referred to me as an expert in the Law or a scholar. This type of stature conferred political leadership as well. The Pharisees not only kept the tradition of Mosaic and Talmudic Law alive and thriving, but the group carried the ambitions of the working class in the political arena. Frankly, I enjoyed my positions of leadership in these realms and relished the opportunity to exert my influence in affairs both religious and secular.

From the very beginning of our movement, the Pharisees held unique beliefs compared to those in the Sadducee group. We believed in the resurrection of the dead and rewards in the afterlife. We also believed in angels and spirits. Not so, the Sadducees. While this may be a general stereotype, most Sadducees were members of the aristocratic, monied or priestly class. Their beliefs relied on the written word of the Torah; they did not believe in the oral tradition. For example, since the Torah did not mention resurrection, the Sadducees argued against our belief about afterlife.

I mentioned that both the Pharisees and the Sadducees represented competing political ideas. The major governing body in Israel was the Sanhedrin. While the Sadducees controlled about sixty-five percent of the seats in this legislative assembly, the Pharisees' position often prevailed because we had the backing of a great majority of the nation's people. As I rose in prominence within the Pharisees, I was appointed to serve in the Sanhedrin. It was a significant honor and I was, quite frankly, very pleased to be given this powerful position. There was one daunting and often discouraging aspect of serving in this body: the two main groups never agreed on anything, so there was a lot of useless political posturing on both sides trying to score hollow political advantage. Why couldn't those idiot Sadducees see and accept the obvious rightness of the Pharisee positions? It never occurred to me that we could possibly be wrong about anything.

There was a real benefit to being in a Pharisee leadership role. I met many other Jews from around Israel who were also influential. One man that especially impressed me was a person named Saul of Tarsus. He was brilliant and totally committed to the Pharisee view of Jewish nationalism that disdained contact or compromise with foreigners especially Gentiles. I felt sure Saul would become a singular leader in our movement in the near future.

It was not uncommon to hear about new prophets springing up around the country. We are a people with a rich religious history. Charismatic young zealots with a Moses complex would often gather a group of followers and begin to advocate some variation of Mosaic or Talmudic Law. Most were like spring flowers that burst forth from the ground only to wither and die a few weeks or months later. The majority of these so-called prophets didn't last too long or gather much momentum. They would quickly find out that it is difficult to live up to their own lofty personal standards or to keep the attention of followers without performing some pretty impressive miracles, healings or cures.

Recently, it came to the attention of the Sanhedrin that a new prophet in Galilee was gaining a substantial following. His name was John the Baptist. While somewhat of a wild man in appearance, John was aggressively preaching a message of repentance and was baptizing hordes of people in the Jordan River. There was an interesting twist to John's message; he claimed that he had been sent merely to announce the coming of the long-awaited Jewish Messiah. Further, John said, the Messiah is among us right now. John had told his followers, I am not worthy to untie the sandal strap of the Messiah. Most of us found the reports to be interesting but not very credible. These fairy tales are often heard but seldom fulfilled. Soon someone else will pop up with a new message.

However, this situation with John started to become more complicated. He recently baptized a man named Jesus. When he did so, a number of people nearby heard a voice from the sky say, this is my beloved son. Are those who reported this incident reliable? Where did the voice come from? Who was speaking? Jesus is reported to be a cousin of John. None of us know what to think of these developments. It is reported that Jesus is also preaching throughout the region and is gathering a large following of disciples. Some of his messages imply that he is the Son of God and the Messiah. The Sanhedrin does not like anything that upsets the status quo; that includes both the Pharisees and the Sadducees. We will continue to monitor closely these events, I assure you.

Ongoing reports continue to paint a picture of Jesus as the leader of a serious new movement. We hear of his frequent cures, healings and miracles; it is difficult to label these reports as exaggeration or hysteria. Jesus seems to be gaining a large number of committed followers. Worst of all, he brands the ruling class as hypocritical, arrogant and out of touch with reality. More than offended, the Sanhedrin sees these statements as a risk to their authority. Be on notice, all who threaten the establishment, you will be destroyed before your menace becomes reality. For the first time in short term memory, the Pharisees and Sadducees united in their concerns about the peril Jesus might pose.

In legislative session, the Sanhedrin decided to send a delegation of three Sadducees and two Pharisees to Galilee to confront Jesus and question him about his basic motives and beliefs. I was selected to be one of the two Pharisees. The delegation traveled north to find Jesus and question him. Frankly, it was our intention to trap him in his speech so that we could brand him as a heretic or usurper. We found him with a large group of his disciples and interested observers. The Sadducee members of our group were the first to pose a question to Jesus. They focused on his views about resurrection. They were sure their cleverly worded question would force Jesus to be vulnerable either way he responded. Instead, he calmly destroyed their arguments and turned their statement back on them. Following that, Jesus ridiculed them for a clear lack of knowledge of scripture and arrogance resulting from their rigid beliefs. The Saducees were humiliated in front of the large crowd and quietly seethed with rage over Jesus' remarks to them. Inwardly, I was chuckling at the discomfort being felt by the Saducees. Now it was my turn to ensnare Jesus. I knew Mosaic and Talmudic Law beginning to end. Every part of the Law was crucial to a clear understanding of our religion. Therefore, I posed a question to Jesus that I felt had no correct answer. I said, Rabbi, which commandment of the law is the greatest? I stepped back, folded my arms and, with a cunning curl on my lip, awaited his reply. Jesus looked directly at me with a kindly expression. He showed neither confusion nor hesitation over the question. Instead he calmly and clearly articulated his answer to the crowd and me: You shall love the Lord, your God, with all your heart, with all your soul and with all your mind. This is the greatest and first commandment, he said. Continuing, he stated; the second is like it; you shall love your neighbor as yourself. The whole law and the prophets depend on these two commandments. Then silence followed.

My mind went blank. I had not expected such a simple, yet complete, answer. Jesus' response sewed confusion in my mind. My strong belief in Jewish nationalism required me to reject any collaboration or significant contact with neighbors. I did not love my neighbor...especially Gentiles...as myself and had no thought about ever doing such a thing. Again, the crowds around Jesus were enthusiastic about his rejoinder to my question. Feeling small, petty and humbled by my encounter with Jesus, I faded back into the large circle of people surrounding him. He had put down both the Saducees and a Pharisee. There will be a price he must pay for such humiliation to powerful people. Mark my word.

For the first time I could remember, the total body of the Sanhedrin was of one accord. Jesus must be stopped. He continued to tell his followers that we were vipers, whitewashed tombs full of decay inside, blind hypocrites that demand adherence to strict laws but do not obey the law ourselves. Jesus was an abomination to us. He had to pay a terrible price for these insults and heretical teaching.

Finally, Jesus made a mistake. He came to Jerusalem to celebrate Passover. He was now on our territory and we were swift to arrest him. We quickly held a trial of sorts. Even though the testimony against Jesus turned out to be very weak, even perjurious, the Sanhedrin convinced Pilate to crucify Jesus. He thought he could be successful challenging us. We showed him where the true power was, with us, not him. Let that be a lesson to others who think they can trifle with the power brokers of Israel. No one has more power than the Sanhedrin. Death is the inevitable result to those who challenge our authority.

To make matters worse, we were informed that Jesus had somehow been restored to life and released from his tomb. His followers claimed he was resurrected. Eyewitnesses reported that he had been seen in several places around Israel speaking to his devoted followers, eating with them and appearing in perfect health except for the wound marks from his crucifixion. Few in the Sanhedrin believed these tales but many reported the stories as true. Will this Jesus never stop tormenting us? While I was agitated by these stories and the growing influence of this dead prophet, I was also sure that all this would soon be forgotten and the name Jesus become but a distant memory.

To my utter surprise, I heard that Saul of Tarsus had suddenly become a vigorous disciple of Jesus. He was even preaching Jesus' message to the Gentiles! This was so astounding to me that I could not believe it at first. Later I confirmed that this was true and Saul—now called Paul—was considered a major leader in this new movement. What a terrible waste of talent! This Paul must have been possessed by a devil. What else could I possibly think?

How many of us have deeply held opinions? No matter how elegantly it is prepared, personally I will not eat eggplant. I do not like it and you can't change my mind. Some devout Lutherans, or Catholics, may say I have many friends who are Methodists or Episcopalians or Presbyterians, but I would never be comfortable worshipping in their churches since our creeds are so different. Democrats cannot fathom the policies espoused by the Republicans, and vice versa. Those who have always owned Ford trucks cannot imagine themselves driving one made by Chevrolet. In more serious cases, some will even shun those of another race as being "too different" to associate with. Like it or not, most of us have some mind-sets that are pretty well set in concrete. Hiliel, in our story, surely exhibits those tendencies. If it is not something I was taught or have learned through experience then I will not accept it. This position creates a terrible situation for us. Our rigid closed mindedness shuts us off from any new or liberating ideas that come our way. Think of the many ways each of us has turned our back on a fresh proposal or concept because it didn't fit our personal model for how things should be. If we shut our minds we may miss some wonderful, serious or important messages. This is especially true in our spiritual life. God speaks to us in whispers. He is always reaching out to us with love, hoping that we will become more intimate with him. What has he said to you recently? Nothing? Perhaps you have your antennae pointed in the wrong direction or your receiver is in the "off" position. It is time for us to tear down the walls around us that block all incoming thoughts, suggestions or signals. As the homilist says, may we have eyes to see, ears to hear and hearts to understand God's messages to us this day.

ZEBEDEE, FATHER OF JAMES AND JOHN
Matthew 4: 21-22

My ancestors lived in Galilee and my wife, Salome, and I have always lived here as well. Fishing in the Sea of Galilee has always provided our source of income. In addition to catching fish, my hired men and my sons, James and John, dry and smoke fish and sell these products throughout the area. We also repair boats and mend nets. Compared to most in our community, we are considered well off. We are diligent about not flaunting our minor wealth; I have always believed in being generous to my neighbors who are in need. We are not conspicuous about our generosity, either. I clearly understand that all this material good fortune is a gift from God and must be treated that way. I have impressed these lessons on my two sons since they were young boys, and I believe they have accepted this idea.

Salome and I have tried to raise our sons as devout and observant Jews. While James and John both have obtained a generally good secular education, neither one of them particularly excelled in Yeshiva. The Torah and Talmud didn't seem to stick with them. It's not that either boy was rebellious or non-religious. On the contrary, they seemed to possess most of the important virtues and were prayerful in their daily lives. Oh, they had their faults like all of us. Both young men could be pretty explosive when their patience ran short. I often had to counsel them about their bad tempers. They tried to overcome this problem, I'm sure, but sometimes it got the better of each of them.

One day John, our younger son, told us he had met an impressive prophet and preacher named John the Baptist. This man was calling for all to repent and prepare for the coming of the true Jewish Messiah. The prophet also said that the Messiah was already living among us. John was enthusiastic about the Baptist and had convinced his brother to join him once or twice to hear the prophet speak. I'm never sure what to think about these men who emerge from the mists occasionally to claim the mantle of God's messenger. I know during the history of our people that many famous and legitimate prophets have played an important role in our religious culture. The problem comes in recognizing which of the many who appear are truly speaking words inspired by the Almighty God we worship. John continued to inform us that he was convinced the Baptist's message was both compelling and true. All of us should be carefully listening to what John the Baptist was saying, my son urgently claimed.

One day our John excitedly burst into our home with the most remarkable news. He had been present at the Jordan River when the Baptist met and baptized a man named Jesus of Nazareth. The two men conversed at some length before the actual baptism took place. After it was completed, John said a number of by-standers clearly heard a voice, seemingly coming from the sky that said, this is my beloved son with whom I am well pleased. No one nearby saw anyone and all were quite amazed at the event. Afterward, there was much discussion among the Baptist's followers about who this Jesus was. Some claimed he was a cousin of the Baptist. Others said that Jesus was the Messiah that the Baptist had repeatedly spoken about. What a thought! Was the long awaited Jewish Messiah actually here? Why were there no current predictions about this from the scribes and religious lawyers? I told my son, John, that there were supposed to be clear passages in scripture that described who the Messiah would be and how he would be recognized. Why was no one speaking about this issue if the Messiah was truly among us now? I was exhilarated, confused and wary as we continued this conversation.

Several weeks later, my two boys and our hired hands were preparing to dock our boats, store the fish we had caught in barrels and put away our nets for the day. This was a busy time and all of us were very engaged in the last minute activities that would conclude our day of work. Now that I was older, I left most of the heavy jobs to my sons and the hired men. I exited over the side of my boat and waded the last few feet to the shore. There I found a small group of people gathered around a tall, handsome man. His face was angular with wide set eyes; he had a quick and easy smile and seemed to be enjoying his casual conversation with the few people around him. He was obviously the center of their attention. When he spotted me walking up the beach, he broke away from the group and walked toward me. As we came close together, he extended his hand to shake mine. I am Jesus of Nazareth, he said. I am very pleased to meet you, Zebedee; I have heard much about you and your generosity to this community. Odd; he knew my name. I told Jesus that I had heard about him through my son, John, and recounted that my son had witnessed his encounter in the Jordan with the Baptist. With a ready smile, Jesus told me that day had been very important to him. After a couple of additional pleasantries, Jesus grew more serious. Zebedee, he said, I have need of your sons, James and John, to help me with my ministry. There is most important work I must do, and it will require the help of many including your boys. To give them up to me will be a sacrifice for you. I understand this clearly and I thank you now for your generosity in allowing your sons to join my work. Just as Jesus finished this thought, my sons came up the beach beside me hauling some of our nets. Jesus greeted both James and John and then said to them, matter-of-factly, come, follow me. Without turning to even say a goodbye to me, my boys dropped the nets where they stood and began walking up the beach, one on each side of Jesus.

I felt desolate, alone and afraid watching my sons departing into the twilight. A couple of my hired men came up to me and asked, what happened to James and John? I...don't...know, I whispered, fighting back tears. I couldn't let my employees see me this way. I brushed away the tears and began shouting orders about the nets, how to handle the barrels of fish and getting the boats properly tied up. I was doing my best to hide my broken heart. My beloved James and John! Where have you gone? Will I see you again? Who is this Jesus? How has he so quickly and easily captured your affections and loyalty? That evening, at home with Salome, I wept as I explained to her what had happened. I felt as if I had lost my two sons as surely as if they both had drowned in the sea on the same day. I felt empty.

While the fishing business needed a major overhaul without James and John to provide daily help, my worst fears did not happen. We often saw the boys when they passed through Bethsaida. They were obviously very happy following Jesus and had both taken on a seriousness about his mission and their part in helping it grow and touch people's hearts and minds. My sons regaled their mother and me with the stories about Jesus' cures, his ideas and the miracles he was performing. Neither boy was subject to exaggeration so we accepted what they were telling us as true. Jesus was surely the greatest prophet I had ever heard or read about. Where will this lead my sons, I wondered? I got a good laugh during one of their visits when they told me that Jesus was now calling them *boanerges,* which means "sons of thunder." Obviously, their association with this holy man, Jesus, had done little to solve their human weakness of bad temper. It sounded to me like Jesus just might be a very good judge of character!

We missed our boys immensely. Each time we had a fleeting visit with them, they seemed to be more mature spiritually. Jesus was influencing them, to be sure, and I couldn't help thinking it was for the better. Still, if we could only have them come back home to us.....

How hard it is for us to have wisdom when dealing with our children or grandchildren. Most parents want the best for their kids but it is difficult not to control their choices rather than guiding them to make good decisions for themselves. We see our children—at almost any age—as lacking the judgment or maturity to handle tough situations on their own. So, with good intentions the parents offer unsolicited advice about how things should be managed. The predictable reaction? "Please, mother and father, I want to handle this myself!" If the parents are wise, they back off, say a prayer, cross their fingers and let the child reach his or her own decision. Guidance and advice from the elders may have a place in this process but not demands or orders to the younger person.

Zebedee represents a classic example of the conflicted parent. While hearing, and hoping, that what he is being told by his sons about Jesus is true, the father has no way of knowing how this situation is going to turn out. He is unaware, for example, that James will become the first apostle martyred by the sword of Herod Agrippa in just a few years. Or that Jesus will be resurrected from his tomb and proclaimed as the Son of God. He cannot predict that John will become a leading apostle and will chronicle much about Jesus and the early days of the church. Parents face this same murky view of how things will turn out for their kids. Like Zebedee, all parents must be willing to turn over their children to God at some point. As Kahlil Gibran wrote in <u>The Prophet</u>, "God has no grandchildren." Let God take care of your children since they are also His children. Have you yet offered your children up to God's care? If not, do you think it might be time to do so now?

SIMON THE LEPER
Matthew 26: 6-7

I am the most fortunate man on earth. As a teenager I contracted the terrible disease of leprosy. On every level of life, this malady brings unimaginable pain and agony to those who have it—physically, psychologically, emotionally and spiritually. Grotesque disfigurement may be the least of leprosy's effects. The cruelest outcome is loneliness and abandonment. No one has any idea how the illness is transmitted but everyone believes it is highly contagious and probably passed by physical contact. When a person shows the first signs of the disease, it is common for the afflicted one to be sent out of the home and village to a remote colony of other lepers, there to scavenge desperately to eke out bare survival. Minimal food and shelter, no medical assistance and lack of basic requirements for a decent life make these leper colonies horrible places in which to exist. People are routinely found hanged because suicide becomes a viable option to the person without hope.

My anguish was made worse by being ripped away from my loving mother, father and siblings who loved me very much and whom I adored. I also could not bear to part with my close cousins Mary, Martha and Lazarus who lived nearby our home in Bethany. In normal times, I had almost daily contact with them and we shared every aspect of our lives with one another. When I got the ghastly news of my condition, I was devastated to think I might never see my immediate and extended families again or my circle of friends. Can you possibly imagine the ache in my heart when contemplating such a possibility?

At first, my symptoms were light and I hoped that I might find something that could reverse the disease entirely. But, watching the progress of the disease in others soon disavowed that hope. Like most of the other lepers, I became increasingly worse. Hands, feet, ears and facial features, like my nose, became appalling to look at. By my early twenties, I had joined the majority of lepers who had pretty much lost hope of ever returning to society. Life, as I had known it, seemed over to me. In my woe, I lashed out at God. We Jews believe that bad things only happen to bad people as punishment. What had I possibly done to deserve such a horrifying existence? God has been grossly unfair to me and I began to hate Him for how I was being treated.

During my forced exile, my cousins regularly sent me letters via the food and water delivery couriers. They always tried to be cheery but I saw through their upbeat communications. Deep down, they knew I was in terrible condition and living in a human *gehena*. While I'm sure they still loved me, my absence made it harder for them to identify with my miserable existence. That realization cast me into further sadness and depression...as if I needed another reason to feel sorry for myself.

After a long silence, I received a letter from my cousin, Lazarus. He wrote that many in Galilee had been introduced to a wonderful new prophet named Jesus from the town of Nazareth. This Jesus was different, Lazarus wrote; his ideas were fresh and inspiring. He was also performing many miracles and curing the sick throughout the region. Along with his sisters, Mary and Martha, Lazarus said they had become devoted disciples of Jesus, often having him in their home. Lazarus continued, Simon, I have asked Jesus to travel to the place where you are living. I believe he has the power to cure you of leprosy. Please pray that you may be granted the grace to believe in Jesus as we do so that he might make you well. I love you, my brother.

Once hope is shattered in pieces like a broken pot, it is not easy to put it back together. On a basic human level, I wanted to believe that a miracle cure was possible. Perhaps my cousin's friend possessed some magical powers. But fifteen years of living with lepers and leprosy had left me bitter and cynical about a better future. Experience had taught me there were no human cures and death provided the only final relief from this dreaded condition. Yes, I wanted to believe and even prayed as Lazarus had suggested. No chorus of angels appeared to validate my prayers. The only response to my prayer was the moans of my fellow lepers as we sat on the dunghill of our colony. God must be dead, I thought.

A few days later, we noticed an uncommon sight on the road near our commune. There was a large group of people approaching us. We had been told by the authorities to avoid any contact with travelers, but I felt compelled to get a closer look. Coming near the road, I saw Lazarus along with others walking with a man I did not know. I was now about twenty yards away from the group. I did not think Lazarus would recognize me because of my disfigurement so I called out, Lazarus—it is me, Simon. He cried out in joy: Simon, O Simon! I have brought Jesus here to meet you. With that, Jesus broke away from the group and walked toward me. He never appeared revolted by my ugly visage but kept his eyes directly on mine. Then Jesus did a most remarkable thing: he put out his hand and touched my face! No one had touched me in over fifteen years! I dropped to my knees and burst into tears. His gentle contact was the most humane thing I had ever experienced. Quietly, Jesus said to me, Simon, I know you are in great distress. Your spirit is torn apart because of your hatred for God and your body is ravaged by leprosy. Do you believe that I can cure your soul and body? I desperately wanted to believe this man standing in front of me. But he was a mere human just like me. How could he possibly cure me both in body and soul? I thought, he is a friend of Lazarus who described Jesus as a holy prophet. What should I do? What should I say? God, I begged, give me the words I should use. I looked up to Jesus and, through my sobs said, please, Jesus make me whole again both in soul and body. He smiled down at me, his hand still resting lightly on my cheek, and said to me, Simon, I will that you be made well in body, mind and spirit. Now return to your colony, lie down and go to sleep. What else must I do to be cured, Lord, I asked? Jesus, still smiling, said to me, do what I have told you.

He returned to the road and I turned and headed back toward the hovel I called home. I didn't feel any different; I didn't look any different. Was this to be some cruel hoax played on me? I couldn't believe Lazarus would do such a thing to me. I did lay my head down on a pile of rags while my mind continued to race. I was so drained and exhausted by this encounter with Jesus that I quickly fell into a deep sleep.

I must have slept through the whole night. It was the cusp of dawn when I awoke. I was slightly disoriented. In the dark gray light, I could make out nearby shapes but nothing more. Then I held out my hands. The leprosy was gone! Kicking off my blanket, I saw my feet. Cured! I felt my face with my restored fingers. I was fresh, whole, perfect! God be praised! The others were still asleep. I leapt up and began running up the hill to the road. I kept on running toward the direction of home as the sun came up, all the while continuing to examine myself. Running, then walking, and running some more until Bethany came into view. It was now around 8:00 in the morning. The home of Lazarus, Mary and Martha was closer to the edge of town than our family's house. My mind was a delirious blur. I knocked on the front door. Mary opened the door and shrieked in amazement as she recognized me. Martha and Lazarus rushed to join Mary and all four of us dissolved into a group hug. It was the happiest moment of my life. Finally, I said, where is Jesus? Come, Lazarus said, he is having breakfast in the back of the house. I found him sitting at a table, some fruit and bread on the plate in front of him. I dropped to my knees next to where he sat. With my voice shaking and my eyes full of tears, I said, O, Jesus, my Lord, I can never thank you enough for what you have done for me. I am eternally grateful for being freed of my leprosy, I also feel somewhat afraid because I don't know who you are or how you cured me...but I shall never forget your kindness for what you have done. What can I possibly do for you in return? Beaming, Jesus reached down and tousled my hair and said, get up and sit next to me on this bench. He gave me a piece of the fruit on his plate and said, Simon, I have been sent by my Father to cure the world of its illnesses. Healing the physical body is easy. Fixing the soul is often more difficult. I can see your body is restored. How about your soul, he asked?

I had been so focused on my physical transformation that I had not thought much about my inner feelings. Before the cure, I hated my physical condition and I hated God for allowing me to have leprosy. Was I over my harsh feelings for God? Perhaps, but I knew my heart would take more time to heal. I told Jesus, while my body is restored I need your grace and prayers to completely return my soul to spiritual health. Will you help me, Jesus? Of course, Simon, he said, you will be completely well soon. I grabbed his hands and brought them to my face then covered them with kisses. Finally, I threw my arms around his neck and kissed his cheek with the same gesture of love he had used when he touched my cheek yesterday.

Word of my arrival spread quickly. As I left my cousins' house, I could see my family running up the road to welcome me home. It was a glorious reunion. It took me several hours to unfold the entire story but I savored every word that I spoke to them. The next day, my mother and father allowed me to have a party for my cousins. Jesus was also invited as the guest of honor. Finally, my cousins asked if they could bring a new friend, Mary Magdalen. This woman previously was known as a prostitute in Bethany but became a disciple of Jesus and had totally reformed her life. It was a wonderful party, full of emotion and interesting little twists. I was home! I was healed! All glory and honor to Jesus of Nazareth the great prophet. I owe everything to him.

All human beings, if they live long enough, endure some difficult patches in their lives. Disappointment in love, a failing grade in an important class, defeat in a student election or a minor fender-bender auto accident are small examples of the many ways life can deal us a losing hand. After facing these minor problems, most of us can pick ourselves up, dust off the hurt or distress and trudge on leaving our troubles behind. But what of the major, tragic events that afflict so many. How can we possibly deal with a shattering divorce, the promising child who becomes a victim of drug addiction, the diagnosis of a life-threatening illness, the total estrangement of a close loved one or the sudden death of a spouse? Such catastrophic incidents often shatter our once solid emotional or spiritual foundation leaving us broken, confused, angry and trusting neither man nor God.

Simon experienced this when diagnosed with leprosy. He had lost hope both in his cousins and in God. Even though we may believe, just as Simon did, that God has abandoned us we must continually remind ourselves that is not true. God dwells within each of us all the time. He is there not just when we are happy or feeling good about life. He is also there and loving us unconditionally when we are in the depths of despair, crushed by life's circumstances or terrified by an impending disaster. Many of us have had moments in life when we felt hopeless. When those times occur, we must humbly turn to our loving God and say: I feel alone, abandoned and afraid. Give me the grace of hope. Let me feel your presence in my life. Wrap me in your loving embrace and let me understand that "this, too, shall pass." Thank you, Lord.

PERES, THE SERVANT MAID
Matthew 26: 69-72
John 18: 25-27

 Am I bitter about life? I suppose you could say that. It seems to me that every one of my twenty-two years has been hard. I feel like I have lived every moment in a barren desert buffeted by strong winds and blowing sand that take another layer of skin off every day. No, nothing has been easy and very little that I can recall has even been pleasant. I have lurched from one hard scrabble situation to another. It is only recently that hope has come into my life. I'll tell you more about that later. But, first, let me briefly recount the circumstances that have brought me to where I am today. Unfortunately, it's mostly an unpleasant story.

 I was born in Jericho north of Jerusalem. Little children seldom know for sure but as I grew, I learned my parents were very poor. It seemed to me that each day presented a new crisis about what we would eat or wear and what my father would do for work. He was a day laborer who departed for the village square early each morning hoping to be hired that day. I remember him telling us about working in the fields and vineyards or helping with building projects of one sort or another. It was a good day if he found employment. Many days saw him coming home empty handed. He never said the words but I'm sure he felt a sense of discouragement and failure about his inability to take care of the family's material needs. He would often show his frustration by lashing out physically at his wife and his children. We kids often prayed that father would return home with a shekel or two in his pocket so he wouldn't manifest his failure by abusing us. As you can imagine, my father was not a very happy man.

Mother was a quiet, subdued and submissive woman. I'm sure her daily life left her feeling beat down and hopeless. I cannot recall ever having an extended, pleasant conversation with her. Our talks always seemed perfunctory and focused on the minutia of daily survival. Observing my mother one day when I was a teenager I thought to myself: is this all I have to look forward to? What a grim future that would be, I mused.

At age sixteen, I believed I had found a way out of the depressing life I was living. A young man named Isaac in our neighborhood began to take a real interest in me. With less than subtle encouragement from me, this casual relationship turned into a real courtship. Just six months after I met him, Isaac formally asked my father for my hand in marriage. Isaac had few of the physical or personality characteristics that would make him a sought after groom. He was actually a little shorter than I and of a slight, almost frail, physique. Bland would be the best word to describe his personality, and he possessed no particular skills that would assure our financial future. To me, his most important asset was availability—I could use him to exit my miserable existence and go off to build a better life. Obviously, this was not a solid basis for getting married, but to me it looked like the chance of a lifetime.

I had just turned seventeen when we were married. Initially, we lived in a detached building on his father's property but within a year Isaac had managed to find a very small house of our own. By that time I was pregnant. My husband did not inspire me in any way, but I did admire his work ethic. He was doing his best to provide for us, and I found him to be respectful towards me which I deeply appreciated. Our life together was not easy, but it was better than anything I had known. When I saw my mother, I could tell that she was envious of my situation.

I did rely on mother for advice and counsel as my pregnancy reached term. Like any woman, I had many apprehensions about giving birth and then caring for an infant. I suppose that unease is part of human nature. I had often wondered how a mother of three, four or five children was able to deal with the various issues she had to face each day as she raised so many kids. Well, I soon learned about the rigors of giving birth and caring for a child, at least one. I was anticipating my new role with joy.

As all mothers discover, birthing a child is very hard work indeed. When a new life is finally brought forth into the world successfully, a mother's pain and discomfort is replaced with wonder and a feeling of happiness to hold her healthy new baby. At least, that was my experience. Isaac was there with me as we welcomed a little girl into our family. Just moments after our child was born, I vowed that she would have a better childhood than I had experienced if I could help it.

Several months later, Isaac found himself on a team of workers going north to Damascus to help build a bridge. He was told to plan on being away from home for about three months. Up till then, we had shared responsibility in caring for our little baby girl. I hated to see him go but knew this was a very good economic opportunity for Isaac. I wished him luck as he headed to Damascus. Silently I prayed that I would be able to care for the baby on my own and brave enough to survive alone while Isaac was away. During his absence, we experienced a violent thunder and lightning storm that also produced a lot of hail. Our roof was damaged by this hail and I asked our mutual friend, John, to come by and do what he could to fix the problem. I was so grateful for his help. He completed the required repairs and our roof was back intact. For all his assistance, I baked a small sweet cake for John and gave him an appreciative little kiss on his cheek as he headed back to his own home. I was really thankful that my roof had been restored.

Isaac finally returned, about ten days later than planned. He was exhausted from the journey and all the work but brought home a leather sack full of money that he had earned. I had never in my life seen such a large sum. After taking off about a week to restore his energy, Isaac went back to his normal work. It seemed that our routine was re-established; everything was proceeding well. Then, one night Isaac came home in a silent, sullen mood. After dinner, I asked him what was bothering him. He said to me, you know what the problem is; your relationship with John. I was shocked by this comment. I had no relationship with John other than as a mutual friend of Isaac and mine. What can you possibly mean, I asked Isaac? He snarled back at me, several people saw you kissing John when he visited our house in my absence. What do you have to say for yourself? I couldn't believe this was happening. I am totally innocent, I cried. When John came to repair our roof, I baked him a sweet cake and gave him a friendly kiss of thanks on the cheek as he prepared to return home. That is all—there was nothing more, I said, my voice shaking. Well, I don't believe you, Isaac stated. You have never really loved me and I'm not surprised that you have had your eyes on John all along. You have dishonored my home, Isaac snapped, and I want you out of here by tomorrow night. His words tore my heart in half. I had never been unfaithful to Isaac, even in my fantasies. How could he be so cruel to throw me out of his home on such flimsy evidence?

I knew that men dominated the society and women are considered as chattel, second-class citizens and worse. If Isaac stubbornly refused to listen to my side of the story, there was little I could do to protect my interests. If he wanted me gone, I was gone and I had no higher authority to appeal to. I virtually had the status of a serf or slave, and all Jewish law and tradition was on the man's side. I was doomed. Suddenly, I felt consigned to hell and the future for my baby and me was unimaginably depressing. What would I possibly do now?

Isaac's decision was rigid and final. I was forced to skulk back to my parent's home with my baby and beg for a place to stay. With the greatest reluctance, they agreed I could stay for a short while until I made more permanent arrangements. Of course, I was shunned and humiliated by the community. In the eyes of most, Isaac must have divorced me with cause; therefore, I was considered to be a scarlet woman guilty of adultery or worse. How could I possibly support my baby and myself in this situation? Jobs were scarce but I had to find one—and in a hurry. My parent's situation was no better than it had been so they were not able to support me even if they wanted to. At best, mother could supply babysitting while I looked for work.

I could find nothing in Jericho. I traveled south to Jerusalem hoping there would be something in that very large city. Finally, I heard of an opening for a courtyard maid at the palace of the high priest. I rushed over there and spoke to the head servant. He agreed to hire me to keep the courtyard tidy. Since this area was used by all supplicants trying to see the high priest, as well as their animals, this was sure to be a dirty, stinking job. But the job was steady and the pay, though a pittance, was enough for me and my baby to eat and keep a roof over our heads. I retrieved my baby from my parent's home, and found a small room to rent in Jerusalem in the home of a woman who agreed to care for my child while I was at work. My dream of economic and social liberty when I married had vanished. It seems that I had returned to a dead end, depressing and hopeless way of life. Would it last forever?

The job? It was worse than I imagined. Dirt, filth and animal waste was everywhere. It was a never-ending job to clean it up and I could not stay ahead. At the end of each day, I was a smelly mess not fit to be near. And tomorrow would be a repeat of today and worse perhaps. Had it not been for my sweet baby, I feel sure I would have ended my life because this was no way to live. I wondered: was I cursed with misfortune? Would I ever experience sustained happiness? What could I possibly do to change the direction of my life? I had no idea what to do. Then I heard about a young prophet named Jesus of Nazareth. He was preaching a message about hope for the poor. He was preaching about me and my baby.

I had not seen Jesus, just heard about him from co-workers and acquaintances. He was gaining a large following of disciples up north in Galilee, but his fame was quickly spreading south too. He not only spoke of love, peace and caring for others, but he was quick to condemn the community leaders for their blatant hypocrisy. I easily identified with that theme. My own experiences taught me that men, especially when in a power position, were manifestly hypocrites. Though I had never been a religious person, everything I heard about Jesus led me to believe I could become a follower of this man. I frequently spoke to visitors at the palace, asking about Jesus and gaining further insight about his ideas. The more I learned, the more intrigued I became. Then I heard that Jesus was coming to Jerusalem next week. I was excited; perhaps I would actually get to meet him, I thought.

It was a Sunday when Jesus arrived. I could not believe the enthusiasm of the welcome he received. I was not working that day but stood along the side of the street where Jesus rode a donkey into town as the folks clapped, cheered and lay palm branches on the road in front of him. He was being treated like a king! I couldn't help thinking this would not be pleasing to the high priest since such a display certainly represented a threat to his power in the community. Jesus passed nearby and I made fleeting eye contact with him. He was a tall and handsome man with a ready smile and a face full of expression. When he looked at me, he smiled; I was thrilled even though I did not speak to him or have physical contact. I was mesmerized!

I was right about the high priest and all of his cronies. Jesus both worried and frightened them. You could feel tension rising in the city during the week as Jesus attracted more attention. I was on duty Thursday night when suddenly there was a big commotion outside the palace gates that quickly spilled into the courtyard. Jesus was being dragged into the palace by a large contingent of soldiers and was followed by many citizens. Jesus had been viciously beaten, and staggered as he was pulled by the military personnel. He halted right next to where I was standing as someone went to get the chief priest. Jesus' breath was rapid and shallow, his unfocused eyes fluttering as blood dripped down his face from wounds on his head. He turned and looked directly at me. We meet again, he said. I remember seeing you last Sunday when I came into the city. I could scarcely believe Jesus was speaking to me. What have they done to you, I groaned to him? What did you say that evoked their wrath, I asked? In a husky voice, Jesus said to me, don't worry about me; what is happening to me must be done. Peres, I want you to shake off the gloom and despair you feel in your life. Instead I call upon you to embrace the good news that I have preached and become one of my disciples. Can you do that, he asked? With my heart racing and softly crying, I responded, yes, Jesus, I will do my best. Now, what can I do for you? He smiled gently at me and said, do not let your heart be troubled. My spirit will be with you always. Then, with a cruel tug, the soldiers again pulled him away towards the high priest's office. I never saw Jesus again.

A little while later, I saw a man who I recognized from the prior Sunday walking at Jesus' side. As the man passed me I said to him, aren't you one of Jesus' disciples? I saw you with him recently. He looked at me with fear in his eyes and shouted at me, no, I am not one of that man's disciples. A few feet further on, another maid said to him, surely you are one of that man's followers; even your Galilean accent gives you away. With panic in his voice, the man shouted to the other maid as he raced to the exit, I do not know the man! Suddenly the courtyard became quiet. Just then I heard a cock crow. It was strange. Then the din returned. I wonder who that man was?

I heard that they executed Jesus the day after I spoke to him. Then, wild rumors started circulating that Jesus had been raised from the dead and had been seen by many people throughout Israel. It was obvious that he had made a mighty impression for his following was growing faster each day. Whenever I could, I would attend a session where the ideas of Jesus were shared. Slowly but surely, I became a believer, was baptized along with my little girl and became a member of The Way. This conversion seemed to change my entire outlook on life and soon things started looking better regarding my future. It wasn't long before I found a new position as a maidservant to the wife of a rich cloth merchant. Comfortable quarters for my daughter and I were included as part of my compensation and the job itself was so much more interesting and fulfilling. Yes, through God's grace, my life had changed course both physically and spiritually. That brief encounter with Jesus transformed me. I don't think I will ever be the same person again.

Many of us have experienced a situation where we were unjustly accused of doing something that was bad, incorrect or injurious to another. Have you ever had a supervisor tell you that a job had been screwed up because of your incompetence? The facts may show that you had nothing to do with the problem but no one will listen to your side of the story. Perhaps a relationship with a long time friend was destroyed because you were blamed for starting a rumor about that person. You are eager to clear your name of this false accusation but all minds have been made up. A minor traffic accident is blamed on you for a failure to yield. Yet the facts clearly show the other driver was at fault. Unfortunately, the police report is not favorable to you. In our story, Peres was accused of a major social failing even though the events were entirely innocent. She carried her bitterness and anger with her until she has an encounter with Jesus. Her life as a victim was forever changed. And, so it is with us. At our lowest points in life when everything seems dark, sour and dreadful, we must find a way to turn to our God for consolation and strength. Most of us need to be reminded occasionally that God loves us unconditionally just the way we are at this moment. It is easy to feel that God may have abandoned us just when we need His help most. It takes lots of humility and a generous helping of sincere prayer to rediscover the truth that God is always with us and reaching out to assist us in our most needy moments. Lord, when I feel alone and persecuted, when all I see while looking up is a black cloud, please show me Your presence. I know you will never send me more than I can handle, but I need to know You are there to help me. Whisper Your words of love to me, God, and refresh my soul.

NAOMI, PETER'S MOTHER-IN-LAW
Mark 1: 29 – 39

I have always lived a quiet and relatively uneventful life. Never did I think that I would meet a wondrous prophet sent from God nor have a son-in-law who emerged as a leader of a large movement. These momentous events started when I was about forty years old. Frankly, they overwhelmed my simple life like a whirlwind and left me with mixed and unsettled feelings. I will never understand how I became swept up in this situation. I can tell you that I was profoundly changed by what occurred. Let me take you back a few years to a time before I met Jesus of Nazareth.

My husband, Thomas, and I had a small home in Capernaum very close to the Sea of Galilee. He was a fisherman. His days were long and he worked very hard to earn a living. Some days he would return home at dusk discouraged by his lack of success catching fish to sell. Most of the time, fortune smiled on his efforts. We certainly weren't rich but Thomas did a fine job of providing for our family. We had two children, Amos and Ruth. Both were good kids of whom we could be proud. As he grew to be a teenager, Amos was very helpful to Thomas and often went out in the boat to assist his father. Ruth was a sweet girl, quieter than her brother. She was very willing to pitch in with the household work and was also a good companion during the long days when Thomas was working. I was bemused by how a mother and father could produce two children who were so different in their personalities yet complimented and loved each other—and their parents—very much.

We certainly could not see anything on the horizon that would impose a change on our style of living and working. Thomas and I often spoke about getting older and how we planned to turn over the small fishing business to Amos who was very competent. We also hoped Ruth would find a decent, hard working man to be her marriage partner throughout life. Thomas and I could then live the natural progression of life through our old age and eventual death. Both of us were perfectly content with this scenario. Our major objectives in life were to do a good job raising the children to adulthood as mature, productive and moral people who loved God, their parents and cared for any neighbor who might be in need. What more could one ask out of life? It looked like everything we hoped and planned for was attainable. God is good and bountiful to his chosen people. All praise to our mighty God.

In our community there were a number of families involved in fishing. Amos knew several young men who also assisted their fathers including James and John, Zebedee's boys, and Andrew and Simon from another family. When the boys were not working, they often congregated together to take part in community events. As is typical for young men their ages, most of these gatherings involved meeting young women in some type of social setting. Thomas and I often chaperoned these get-togethers to insure that the contact between the sexes was proper. We really didn't worry too much since all the young people acted in a wholesome and appropriate manner, at least most of the time.

Ruth joined this social scene when she grew to be a young woman. Because she was quite shy, Ruth seemed to hold back a little even though she told me she enjoyed meeting and talking with the boys. I think parents are probably more protective of their daughters since we consider them a little more vulnerable than sons and subject to being hurt in personal relationships. Fortunately, Ruth continued to grow in maturity and exhibited a quiet but firm personality. We were proud of both of our children. Amos had become a strapping young man who was a great help to his father. Ruth was a mature and intelligent young woman who seemed self-assured and in control. They were wonderful, both of them!

I began to notice a subtle change in Ruth. More and more, her conversations with me seemed to focus on her relationship with one man, Andrew's brother, Simon. He also began coming by our home to see Ruth instead of just meeting her at the larger group gatherings. The two of them would often sit in front of the house and talk until it was dark. Simon was a pleasant chap, animated in conversation perhaps a little loud and with a hint of a temper. He seemed to be very respectful of Ruth, was solicitous about her feelings and listened intently when she had a point to make in conversation. After Simon would leave, Ruth often shared her thoughts with me. It was obvious that she was falling in love with Simon. Thomas offered that he knew a moon-struck young man when he saw one. Simon already had fallen in love with Ruth, according to my husband.

The fateful day finally arrived. Simon knocked on our door and asked to speak with Thomas. The young man seemed quite nervous. He and Thomas retired to a small covered porch in the back of our house for their chat. You can guess the content. Simon asked Thomas for Ruth's hand in marriage. This was followed by the obligatory discussions about the dowry, how Simon planned to take care of Ruth, future prospects and all the other formalities engendered by such an occasion. While the conversation was serious, both parties knew they were merely going through the motions. Ruth and Simon had earnestly discussed all these things privately and Ruth accepted Simon's proposal of marriage. When Simon departed, Thomas reviewed the meeting with me and then we called in Ruth to hear what she had to say. Of course, Ruth was very pleased with Simon's initiative and affirmed to us that she loved him and wanted to marry him. We were delighted for her. Simon was a hard working man, a natural leader and had a good future. When Amos heard the story, he teased Ruth incessantly until her cheeks flushed. It was all good-natured and the siblings exchanged a big hug after Amos was through having his fun with her. So, part of the goal Thomas and I set for ourselves had been reached. Ruth would soon be married and we were very happy with the arrangement. Ruth and Simon were complimentary and we felt they would achieve a solid and happy life together. In addition, I would now become a mother-in-law and have a new "son." I liked that idea. Simon would be a nice addition to our family. I prayed that God would bless them both.

All the preparations were made and the actual day of the wedding seemed to arrive quickly. The day was lovely, the service conducted by our rabbi was meaningful and reverent, and the party afterwards was joyful and festive. Everything had gone perfectly and the young couple went off to begin their new life together with our blessings and abundant good wishes.

Life settled back into routine. We frequently saw Ruth and Simon, sharing meals at our home or theirs every week. They seemed to be supremely happy and settling in very well. Sometimes when we went to their place, we were joined by Simon's brother, Andrew. Once in awhile we also saw James or John. Andrew and Zebedee's boys often spoke of their interest in a new prophet named John the Baptist. Israel's history is rich with stories about prophets, some who were real and important messengers of God. Many others also popped up who turned out to be mere pretenders. From the initial discussions, we could not determine which classification fit the Baptist. The stories about him were very interesting, and he did seem to be preaching a heartfelt message to the people, one that was not intended to bring glory upon himself. Simon showed an interest in learning more about the Baptist and promised to join Andrew soon to hear the prophet speak. Thomas and I both had a strong spiritual component to our lives but we shied away from any ostentatious display of our religious beliefs. Weekly attendance at temple was fine but traveling to hear an itinerant preacher was not our style. I guess we thought our relationship with God was a more private and personal matter, not one that was manifested in a large community setting.

Our weekly get-togethers for a meal were increasingly focused on discussions about the Baptist. In addition, the boys were also telling us about another man, a cousin of John the Baptist, named Jesus from Nazareth. Apparently, John was paying great deference to Jesus and had actually identified him to many of his followers as the Anointed One or the long awaited Messiah. Such a claim had enormous consequences for the Jewish people. The real Messiah would be greeted with great joy and triumph, but there was serious danger attached to his arrival as well. While the Messiah was expected to free the Jews from foreign oppression, he would also pose a massive threat both to the Roman and Jewish leaders who held their power based on maintaining the status quo. I found the discussion about the Messiah now being in our midst to be exciting but also ominous. Certainly our comfortable, anonymous lives would be forever altered if these stories about the Messiah turned out to be true.

It was our turn to host a family meal. We were surprised when only Ruth arrived. Where is Simon? I asked. Ruth said, Mother, don't be alarmed. I will tell you the whole complicated story over dinner. As we began the meal, Ruth told us an astonishing tale. Last week, at the end of a workday, Jesus of Nazareth was at the shore waiting for the fishing boats to arrive. When all the day-end work was completed, Jesus approached Andrew and Simon. At the conclusion of their brief conversation,

Jesus said to the brothers, come after me and I will make you fishers of men. Walking up the beach a little further, Jesus also talked to James and John and essentially said the same thing to them. In just a few short moments these four men committed themselves to following Jesus and working in his ministry. Ruth reassured us that she totally supported Simon's decision and indicated that she and Simon had great faith that this was part of God's plan for their lives. With candor Ruth said she wasn't sure how this would all work out but she was not worried and had a deeply held belief that this was the right thing to do. Naturally, I was upset and worried for Ruth after hearing the story. How would Simon support her if he wasn't fishing? Was he going to be absent for long periods of time? What if the authorities disapproved of Jesus' ministry? These questions swirled in my head and I voiced my fears to Ruth. Relax, Mom, Ruth said. Everything is going to be fine. God is with Jesus and us.

I guess I'm just a worrier. This dramatic turn of events shook me to my core. I was concerned for Ruth, Simon and everyone who was associated with Jesus. I could only imagine the worst things taking place. Was that a lack of faith? Perhaps, but it was the way I was conditioned to think about things. The more I thought, the more upset I became. Dear God, I prayed, please take care of Ruth and her husband. I began to experience weakness in my limbs and an overwhelming sense of tiredness. I attributed this to my deep concern about Ruth and Simon. There were days I had trouble getting out of bed. Thomas was frantic with worry about me but had no idea what to do to restore my health. I was in my early forties; was I about to die? Again I turned to God and asked him to restore me to health but I did not improve.

Meanwhile, Jesus and his disciples were roaming Galilee preaching, curing the sick and performing miracles. The whole countryside was abuzz about this new prophet, and each day brought more converts to his message of love for God and neighbor. Ruth frequently visited me and took over my household chores so I could rest in bed. She told me that Jesus, in a light moment, had given Simon a nickname—"Rocky"—because of Simon's flinty and tough personality. Since Rocky, or Rock, translates in Aramaic to Peter, many of the disciples were now calling Simon Peter. I personally didn't think I would ever get used to this new name but Ruth was now always referring to her husband as Peter.

My condition further deteriorated. Fever induced chills debilitated me; I could no longer function as a wife or household manager. God must be preparing me to depart this earth, I thought. Ruth was so loving and caring and did everything in her power to assist me. One day she told me that Jesus was coming to Capernaum and she would insist he come by to meet me. I could muster no enthusiasm about his upcoming visit.

One day, I heard a faint knocking on my front door. From my bed I called, come in, please. Then, standing in front of me I saw Simon, Andrew, James, John and Ruth. When they stepped aside another figure entered the room. He was tall and quite handsome with an easy smile, bright eyes and a confident manner. Naomi, he said to me, I am Jesus, the one who has upset your life and caused you so much worry. I am very sorry that I have affected you this way; it certainly was not my intention to trouble you or bring about difficulty for you. Will you forgive me? Jesus asked in a soft, gentle tone. Of course, I responded. I'm sure it is my own predisposition and not you that has caused me to be ill. There is no forgiveness necessary. I just have been very worried about my daughter and her husband. Taking my hand in his, Jesus bent over my bed, closed his eyes and seemed to pray silently. In a few moments, he looked at me and said, I have called down blessings of healing and health upon you, Naomi. It is my will that you be free from your fever and completely restored to health. What I ask of my Father he will give me. Woman, you are now cured of your illness and restored to health.

I did not know what to think. I felt something like a shiver go through me from head to toe. Suddenly, there was a surge of energy throughout my body. I sat up on the side of my bed. I no longer experienced any fever or weakness. On the contrary, I was my old self, full of energy and life. Jesus offered his hand to help me stand up. When I did, there was no trace of my prior debilitation. My God, I thought, this man has completely cured me! Who is he? Where did he derive these powers? The others in the room were laughing and clapping with joy, hugging each other because of the blessing they had just witnessed. How do you feel? Jesus asked. What could I say? After a pause of a few seconds, I said, thank you, Jesus, for what you have done for me this day. Our God has blessed you with mighty powers. I am profoundly grateful that you have used this power to cure me of my illness. Thank you and may God bless you abundantly.

I was excited to be able to return immediately to my role as a hostess to guests. While all the visitors gathered on our rear porch, Ruth helped me as I quickly prepared food for our visitors. It was a long time since I had the opportunity to organize a feast and I enjoyed every minute doing this work.

The story of Jesus' three year public ministry, his crucifixion, death and resurrection and the continuation of his movement led by my son-in-law, Peter, have been well reported by others. You don't need to hear all this again from me. I do want to tell you what my initial encounter with Jesus meant to me. Based on all that subsequently occurred, I believe Jesus is the Messiah and the Son of God. To comprehend fully my first meeting with him is beyond my imagination. There I was, sick in bed and *God Made Flesh* took my hand, prayed over me and cured my illness. The thought leaves me speechless.

Was it really true! Did it really happen? I know that it did; I'm just having a hard time believing it. Can you understand what I am saying?

What does compassion mean? Webster's says it is a strong feeling of sympathy or sorrow for another person's pain or illness and a desire to do something to help alleviate the problem. When thinking about your own life, is compassion part of your personal makeup? Those who have dealt with the serious sickness of a family member, child or grandchild have probably experienced compassion. We can feel the pain our loved one is enduring and would do anything we could to make it end. But, as sacred scripture says, "...even the pagans take care of their own." What about our feelings for the parents of suicide bombers in the mid-east who lose their children in violent deaths? What feelings do we have for the families of people who are convicted of being serial pedophiles? Can we find compassion for men sentenced to death for the brutal rape and murder of innocent children? Do you find it easy to have sympathy for a friend who is a falling down drunk and won't seek help for his or her addiction?

Jesus gave us an example of compassion when he visited Naomi and cured her of illness. We are called to be compassionate people as well. Exercising this virtue is relatively easy when our compassion is directed to one we know and love. The same cannot be said about strangers who do not seem deserving of our compassion. The question is this: are we permitted to withhold our care for others just because of the way they act? Do we really believe that God loves every human being unconditionally? Do we really believe that we are all members of the Body of Christ? An affirmative response to those questions requires us to think in a different way. It may not be easy, but it is required.

TELES, THE MAN WITH A WITHERED HAND
Mark 3: 1-5

    Can you possibly imagine trying to lead a normal, productive life with only one hand? Things irreparably changed for me when, at age twenty-one, my hand was violently crushed in a terrible accident. It was my right hand, the one I favored for all activities like writing, eating and a thousand other little chores that I completed each day. The damage I sustained was so extensive that my hand has hung limply at my side ever since, of no use to me whatsoever. Until one day, that is. But let me finish the rest of my story first and then I will tell you about what happened to me one fateful day when my hand was restored for me.

    I was born and raised in a little village near Capernaum close to the Sea of Galilee. My mother and father had a small home there and after I married, my wife and I continued living in the same community. I recall my childhood as being a happy time. Our family had many friends and relatives living in the area so I remember lots of shared activities, community ball games and early evening meals consisting of fish cooked over charcoal on the beach. My father was a cooper, a man who manufactures barrels. They were used to store a variety of products so the demand was usually pretty steady.

    One day a deliveryman pulled into our yard with a cart full of barrels. Each container was about thirty inches high and contained nails that had been forged by another craftsman. My father had ordered a barrel of nails for use in our work. There must have been about fifteen barrels on the cart for subsequent delivery to other shops that were making wood products or building houses. I reached up to grab a barrel and unload it. When I did, I twisted my foot on a small rock and fell onto the back of the cart. The barrel I had been holding to unload pulled me down—it was heavy—and my fall raised the front end of the cart. This caused the remaining barrels to tumble out of the cart and several of them landed on me lying on the ground behind the cart. I must have been hit by at least one thousand pounds of barrels and nails. The bulk of the containers fell on my right hand and arm as I was pinned under the cart. The immediate pain was excruciating and I cried out in agony. My father ran out of the shop. He and the cart driver frantically pulled the barrels off me. I never lost consciousness during the event. When all the barrels were removed, I could look down and see that my lower right arm, wrist and hand had been severely injured. I was bleeding profusely and it was obvious that most of the bones in my extremity and fingers had been broken. After the initial shock wore off, I became dizzy and started feeling faint. I could hear a group of friends and neighbors working over me trying to staunch the flow of blood. The pain had now become almost more than I could bear. Finally, I passed out.

When I drifted back to consciousness, I was laying on a mat inside my father's shop. My lower arm was completely encased in a blood soaked bandage. I experienced a continuous throbbing pain that seemed to course through my entire body. My worried father was crouched over me, gently wiping my face with a cool cloth. How bad is it? I asked. I do not want to deceive you, son, father responded. Your injury looks to be very severe. You have been examined by a physician who told me that the injuries to your wrist and hand are very serious, father whispered in a choked up voice. I am so sorry, he continued; I wished it had been me rather than you.

My arm and hand were tightly wrapped for several weeks as the injuries healed. Disquieting pain had been replaced with a dull numbness. About six weeks after the original incident, the tight wrap was removed. The wounds to my flesh were healed. Some broken bones were reset but most had not knitted together properly. When I tried to use my hand for simple chores like holding a cup of water or grasping a hammer, I found this part of my body was useless. I wept bitter tears realizing I was never going to get any better. How would I be able to work? Would I be pitied and an object of children's scorn because I was "different" from other men? Would my wife and family continue to love me when I was no longer a functioning and productive member of society? I had a great sense of foreboding about the future.

    I returned to work and tried to be helpful but there were few jobs I could do. Retraining my left hand to do simple things seemed impossible. Father was patient but was finally forced to hire a man to help him. This left me with a few menial tasks such as sweeping the floor. With great sadness, father told me that he was forced to reduce my pay. The business could not support three people with full incomes. Since my ability to contribute was now so limited, he could not continue to operate as before.

    The physical situation was bad enough. Although somewhat healed, I was in constant pain. Now I was becoming seriously wounded emotionally and psychologically. Self-pity was my primary mind set. My wife finally grew tired of this. Teles, she said, you must stop this constant whining about how unfairly life has treated you. Go down to the temple area and observe those who are blind, crippled or terribly disfigured. Perhaps you will then see that your disability is minor compared to many others. It is time for you to snap out of your gloom, she angrily demanded. I did not like to hear that from my wife but, deep down, I knew she was right. What is the justification for constant complaining when nothing can be done to alleviate the situation?

    While I was not irreligious, I was a lukewarm member of the temple. I would attend when it was convenient for me but I was not considered a regular congregant. My accident had not engendered a conversion experience for me, but I did begin to attend temple more consistently at the urging of my wife. She suggested that prayer might help overcome the depression that was parching my spirit. I followed her advice but did so with restrained enthusiasm; all the prayer in the world was not curing my withered hand. Actually the frequent temple meetings had a somewhat negative effect too. I was reminded how hypocritical some of the prominent members were. I saw ostentatious prayer and contributions to the temple treasury by the same people I knew were short-changing customers in their stores or being unfaithful to their wives. Whom do these people think they are fooling? God cannot be deceived, can he? In spite of all these spiritual obstacles, I continued my regular visits to the temple. However slight, I began to feel that my private prayer was helping me develop a better relationship with God. That had to be a good thing, I thought.

I'm sure you have already heard about the new itinerant preacher in our region, Jesus of Nazareth. I won't bore you with further details other than to say he was getting a lot of attention for the miracles and cures he was performing. I must admit; I was curious about him. I began to have this continuing fantasy. If he had cured so many others, couldn't he possibly cure my hand, too? I recognized these thoughts for what they were—pure fantasy. Still, these ideas did provide a glimmer of hope.

I was told that Jesus was invited to visit our temple and preach on the next Sabbath. I was pleased that I would finally see and hear him in person. I arrived for Shabbat service early, hoping to get a seat close to the speaker's rostrum. When the temple was almost full, Jesus arrived with a small entourage. He mingled freely with the members, greeting some he knew and introducing himself to others. When he reached my place, he put out his hand to shake mine but quickly moved to grasp my left hand when he saw the condition of my right hand. With a friendly smile, he said, my name is Jesus. What is your name? I responded, I am Teles. I have heard much about you, Jesus, especially the cures attributed to you. As you have already noticed, I have a useless hand. I am hoping that you may show pity on me and perform some miracle to restore my hand. Is that possible? Jesus was silent for a moment, then looked intently at me and said, Teles, I may have need of you this day. Please be prepared if I ask you to join me later at the rostrum. Will you do that, he asked? I merely nodded my head affirmatively as Jesus moved on to greet the next member of the temple. I noticed that my heart was beating rapidly and my brow was covered with perspiration. Those few seconds with Jesus had obviously affected me, at least physically. He was powerful, charismatic and intently engaging. I was deeply impressed with Jesus; he was like no other man I had met in my life.

Not everyone in the temple was enthusiastic about Jesus and his preaching. His interpretation of Mosaic and Talmudic law was often radical by contemporary standards. During today's visit, he posed a rhetorical question. Jesus asked, is it lawful to do good on the Sabbath rather than do evil or to save a life rather than destroy it? Neither the head rabbi nor any of the temple elders were willing to answer that question. They knew this led to a logical trap with no escape. Silence fell over the room for an extended period. Jesus stood quietly, his eyes glancing over the congregation. Finally, Jesus said, there is a man here who has a withered hand. What do you think? Is it lawful for me to heal him on the Sabbath? I could hear the low whispers throughout the building. One man cried out to Jesus, if you heal Teles you are defying our laws that have come down from Moses. Jesus looked at me and said, Teles, please come up here and stand beside me. I was wary; what was I getting myself into? But, I did what I was asked and traveled the few feet needed to reach Jesus. Again he gazed over the congregation. Jesus said, assume that I have the power to cure this man. Should I do so, even though it is the Sabbath? I found my heart beating rapidly for the second time. An anonymous voice from the back of the temple cried out, no, do not heal him! It is against the law! I was amazed how calm Jesus appeared even in the face of many agitated temple members. Teles, he said to me, put your right hand on the speaker's stand. When I did so, Jesus covered my hand with part of his cloak. He then closed his eyes, raised his face to heaven and seemed to mouth a silent prayer that lasted but a few seconds. My eyes then locked with Jesus. He smiled and slowly withdrew his cloak that had been covering my hand. When he did so, I looked down at my hand resting on the stand. O, my God, I cried! It is a miracle! My hand looked perfect! I made a fist and flexed my fingers. Everything worked perfectly! Then, a wave of terror overcame me. Who is this Jesus? By what power can he cure my incurable disfigurement? Jesus rested his hand on my shoulder. I turned to the congregation and said, praise be to the Almighty God! I am cured! This Jesus has made me whole! Praise God!

My euphoria was not matched by many in the temple. Most of the people seemed hysterical with fear and hated what had just happened. Jesus had flaunted the Sabbath law with this cure. I heard a voice scream, this can only be the work of the devil! You are evil, Jesus! Leave this sacred place now! The place was in bedlam. Many symbolically ripped their clothes in protest and quickly left the temple as if it were occupied by Beelzebub. In the aftermath, Jesus and I were left near the speaker's rostrum. How do you feel, Teles, he asked? Oh, Jesus, I said, I am so grateful for what you have done, but I also feel afraid and confused. Who are you and by what power have you cured my hand? With his gentle smile, Jesus put his arm around my shoulder and said, Teles, I felt great love and empathy for you. I was happy to restore you to health. Thank you for allowing me to use this cure as an important teaching lesson to the religious leaders in this community. I hope you will now resume your normal life, he told me. More than that, Teles, I ask that you always remember how much God has blessed you. Please be a witness to your community of God's benevolence. If you will to do so, Teles, you can be a wonderful example to your neighbors of God's everlasting love. Will you do that for me, Teles, Jesus asked? Oh, my Lord, I will always speak your name with thanks and love. I can never repay you for what you have done for me this day. I will dedicate my life to praising your name, I told him. He responded, go with my love, Teles. I felt limp and my eyes filled with tears of joy. When I returned home, I could not speak to my wife. I merely held out my hand for her to see and touch. Both of us were choked with emotion as we embraced, silently thanking God for this miracle. In just a few moments, my life was changed forever. I wish I could adequately describe my feelings to you but I cannot. There are no words in my vocabulary to explain the depth of change I experienced.

Perhaps you are thinking that the reflection following this story should be about our need to always give thanks to God for his great generosity to us. While that idea is important, the author sees a message about hardened hearts and hypocrisy. How many of us have become rigid in the way we think about certain issues? Politics are a perfect example. The complete polarization of the U. S. electorate makes compromise about even simple things a virtual impossibility. Both sides have their collective feet in concrete and will not consider any arguments that do not agree with their strongly held beliefs. Various Christian congregations are in the same position, professing shock at the wrong-headed or apostate beliefs of other churches.

People no longer watch television news or visit computer websites to obtain new information. They only tune into programs that reinforce what they already think is true. It seems we have become a nation that is hostile to any input that does not correspond to our "correct" way of looking at things. Contemporary clichés seem to capture the essence of the problem; "it's my way or the highway" or "of course I believe in compromise so long as you're the one giving in to me." Simply put, hypocrisy is saying one thing but doing something entirely different. How many of us are quick to embrace the Body of Christ but then work to deny access to societal benefits to some people in the community? Do any of us decry tax policy and then fudge on our income tax? How many of us preach equal pay for equal work and then discriminate in the businesses we own? Many similar examples could be cited. Yes, all of us may be guilty of some hypocrisy from time to time. The key point is to recognize our own disconnect with reality and correct our thinking when we have veered off the path of fairness and justice. Jesus focused a spotlight on hypocrisy when he encountered it. We should ask God to enlighten and grace us when we wander onto the wrong fork of the road.

ASHSAH, THE WOMAN WITH HEMORRHAGES
Mark 5: 25 – 34

Stories about problems experienced by women in our culture don't get much attention. I'm sorry about that since women make up about one half of the population. Shouldn't women's issues be treated with as much importance as those faced by men? On a specific, personal level I am disappointed that my situation was ignored for a significant portion of my adult life. When you hear my story, I hope you will have some sympathy for what happened to me and understand why I carry a sense of bitterness about the way I was treated.

It is difficult to tell my story without seeming to be a whining, self-pitying complainer. I don't think I am that way really, but as my story unfolds, you will see there are not many positive elements to my personal history. I grew up as one of two girls. I was the younger. My sister Sara was beautiful and possessed an out-going, attractive personality. She could have belittled or ignored me but instead was generous and loving towards me. I admired Sara very much and wanted to emulate her in every way. You see, she was lovely, charming and made friends effortlessly. I was quite plain physically, had a more subdued personality and didn't mingle with others easily. Because we were so different in such a variety of ways, I'm sure others were often surprised to learn that we were siblings.

Our childhood experiences were generally good. While our family was not wealthy, we seldom were denied the basic things of life. Compared to others in our community, we were well cared for and taught by our parents to be grateful for our material plenty. Sara, who was three years older than I, always seemed to attract many friends and had the role of leader in most groups. She often included me in her activities even though I was the baby sister. I tried to keep up with her friends but was usually left in the dust by all but my sister. I don't know if I would have been as generous to her if our circumstances were reversed. As Sara reached puberty, she blossomed into a very beautiful young woman and became the center of attention especially to the young adult males in our community. Again, she had the maturity to handle these boys very well. While she mingled easily with them and enjoyed their company, she also sent a clear message about boundaries. The young men knew there were limits to her friendliness towards them. I observed Sara handling these often tricky circumstances and admired her greatly.

    I shall always be most grateful to my mother for how she dealt with our growing up years. In what I now understand to be an age appropriate way, she carefully prepared us for the physical changes we would encounter as we grew up. Mother always spoke in a matter-of-fact tone and there was no hint of embarrassment as she explained the bodily and hormonal changes we would face. She was also direct in her explanation about the difference in the sexes, the urges we would feel in our teenage years, how babies were conceived and all the related issues that would eventually lead to married life and having families of our own. Everything we were told was always in the context of the sacred nature of marriage and how the family was the central unit of civilized society. Many of our friends were not treated with this directness by their parents. We often heard crazy ideas and silly "facts" stated by the youngsters in our community. Our thorough sex education was a blessing passed on to us by our mother but by our father as well. He tried daily to live out his life as a partner in marriage with our mother. Sara and I admired and loved them both.

Sara reached puberty before me. She would share with me information about her rite of passage. Just like mother, she was straightforward and didn't embellish anything. I was fortunate to have such a loving big sister. Everything that was happening to her would come to me soon enough and I appreciated receiving the advance information and advice from Sara.

When I was twelve years and eight months, I experienced menarche. No matter how much prior information you have, the beginning of your first menstrual cycle is always a surprise and a little unnerving. I knew this was the central event of female puberty and I anticipated the other changes that would affect my body in the months and years ahead. Both Sara and mother comforted and advised me as I proceeded through this important change in my young life. I knew that menarche was usually light and lasted only two or three days. But, this was not the case for me. In addition to some severe cramping, the flow lasted for ten days. When it finally stopped, I found myself extremely tired and listless. Mother was perplexed but concluded that each person is different, so my experience, although unusual, was probably a one-time event. She reassured me that things would most likely be easier and more predictable in the future.

Unfortunately, that didn't happen. Again, I had terrible cramping, a very heavy flow of blood that lasted for almost fifteen days. At the end of my period, I was enervated and lethargic. I felt like I had been held underwater in a lake. When I finally surfaced, I was gasping for breath and very weak. I could tell from mother's expression that she was concerned. Such a difficult siege for a young girl was totally unexpected and outside the norm. Mother suggested we see what happens next month before consulting with a physician. Once more, things were very grueling; the third month offered no sign that events were improving. I recognize that these descriptions about my very intimate physical state create an awkward and uneasy aspect to my story telling. However, I felt it was necessary to explain my condition so you could have a context for the rest of my narrative. I will leave it at this: For the next twelve years, I never once experienced an improvement in my menstrual health in spite of numerous visits to physicians in the surrounding area. I had almost continual hemorrhaging. I was as limp as a piece of string.

    Life continued in spite of this problem. As I passed through puberty to womanhood, I lost my gangly, pre-teenage plainness and developed into a fairly attractive woman. While not nearly as pretty or vivacious as Sara, I did attract some of the young men. When you are thirteen or fourteen, you don't have the maturity or vision to see clearly where relationships can lead. I certainly appreciated the attention I was receiving but at some point in the future, the field of suitors would be winnowed and eventually some man would become serious about marrying me. The thought of having a momentous discussion about marriage totally panicked me. There just is no delicate way of telling someone who professes his love for me about my condition. Society just does not provide a mode for this type of discomfited conversation to take place. Even my mother who was so matter-of-fact about sex and sexuality could only stammer generalities to me about such a talk. Please pardon my frankness: I wondered if I could even consummate a marriage and believed I would probably never conceive a child. How do you explain this to a young man who is in love with you and asking you to marry him? I was depressed thinking I would probably live my life without ever having a family of my own.

    I was raised in a moderately religious home. Mother and father taught us to believe in God, be thankful for our blessings and be caring to others less fortunate than ourselves. We observed the Jewish feast days but not with the zealousness of others in the community. Believe me; I have done a lot of praying since I was afflicted. Does God hear my prayers? My weak faith tells me yes but I don't seem to get much of a response. Where else should I turn? I will continue to ask God to assist me in the trial I am experiencing. One day, I went to the temple to pray. While there, I spoke with one of the elders. He told me about a dynamic new preacher who was traveling throughout Galilee performing miracle cures. I was curious to learn more about this man and what he was doing. I was informed that his name was Jesus bar Joseph of Nazareth. In subsequent conversations with others, I learned that Jesus would be visiting a nearby village in a couple of days. I felt compelled to go see him. Maybe...just maybe...he could help me out of the dire straits I was experiencing. Was I being inordinately hopeful? Probably. But, I had to try something. I didn't think I could continue living my life the way things were. To emphasize my point, this was one of the worst months I had ever endured physically. I felt my life was a shambles.

On the appointed day, I was up early and on the road to our neighboring village. I was trying to arrive before the bulk of the crowd assembled. It was very warm and I was laboring as I saw a large group of people ahead. My unspoken dream of seeing Jesus privately and telling him my story was not going to happen. I caught of glimpse of him in the middle of the throng, people pressing in on him and shouting their supplications. He was virtually a prisoner of the swaying multitude. I aggressively pushed and shoved my way closer to Jesus but was not able to reach him. Someone pushed me down to the ground just as Jesus passed my position. I reached out and touched the hem of his cloak, silently asking God for a cure for my hemorrhages. As my hand brushed against the cloth of his garment I experienced a frisson creating a tingle throughout my body. Jesus and the entire mob of people suddenly came to a halt. He said, I just felt power leaving me; who has touched me? He turned and quickly scanned those around him and then his eyes locked onto mine. Is it you, he asked? Are you the one who touched my cloak? I was terrified! He seemed so stern. I could not lie to him and blurted out my confession. O, Jesus, I said, it was I who touched the hem of your garment. I was hoping that you would cure me of the terrible affliction I have endured these many years. Please forgive me if I have offended you in any way, I sobbed to him. His face immediately softened and he smiled at me warmly. I was still on my knees and he gently put his hands on my shoulders. Daughter, I know you have suffered greatly for a long time, he said. To the best of your ability you have prayed and continued to have faith in God in spite of your difficulties. I want you to live a happy life so I will that you now be cured of this burden you have borne these past twelve years. Go in peace and enjoy good health, he said, as he bent down and gently kissed my cheek.

    I was so exhausted I could barely move. The crowd continued down the road, Jesus in the middle of the group. I was left on my knees feeling weak in body but thrilled in my spirit. What a loving, lovable man I had just met. Was he truly the Son of God as some claimed? I could not comprehend such an idea. Me, meeting God? How could that be possible? I finally got to my feet and headed for home. I had never felt such an energy deficit in my life. When I arrived home, I took my daily hygienic bath. O, my God! My bath water was perfectly clear! I was not bleeding. What had happened to me? Had Jesus cured me? Excitement, disbelief and terror filled my mind. Looking up, I cried out to the heavens, God, help my unbelief! No, this could not be true. I am merely having one day without my affliction. I thought back to this morning: Jesus said to me, you're cured; have a happy life. I lingered in my bath and then, after dressing, slept soundly.

I arose the next morning more refreshed than I had been in recent memory. Still, there was no evidence of bleeding. As I went about my daily chores, I frequently checked if there was a reoccurrence of hemorrhage. None today. None the next day either. I knew I must go and find Jesus to thank him for this cure. I walked many miles but finally found him and his friends down by the Sea of Galilee having a meal on the beach. There were no crowds now, just Jesus and a few followers sharing dinner. I felt awkward about interrupting him, but finally gained my courage and approached him. Jesus, I said to him, I want you to know how deeply grateful I am to you for curing my illness. I don't know who you are or where your power comes from but I know you have changed my life. I may not have the strength or faith to be one of your disciples, but I will always be a faithful follower. He looked at me and said, Ashsah, I am so pleased that you are better. You are a lovely woman and deserve to have a happy life. I will be very joyful to count you as one of those who are my disciples. Do your best to be as loving to others as I have tried to be to you. Thank you for finding me to express your gratitude. That tells me that you are a wonderful woman with a heart full of love. Now, go in peace; I will not forget you, Ashsah.

A lot of things happened to me in the next few years, most of them uplifting and rewarding. I spent the rest of my life trying to be a true follower of Jesus. I did not do that because he cured me; I did that because I came to believe he was the Son of God, the Messiah and the Savior of the world. I love him and I know he loves me, too. How many people can claim to have known Jesus and to have been cured by him of a cruel, debilitating illness? I am one of those people, eternally grateful for the experience. Thank you, Jesus, my Lord, for having loved me.

Many of us find ourselves in a prison. We spend our lives locked up with our fears, our failures, our doubts and our weaknesses. The current cliché is that some of us spend our lives in quiet desperation. We are uninspired by our employment, feel unfulfilled in our interpersonal relationships, believe we have failed to reach our potential and do not have real purpose or meaning to our lives. How depressing! In truth, much of this ennui is based on a failure to recognize the presence of God in our daily life. We continue to think that God is "out there" someplace instead of feeling His presence within us. Why is it so hard for many of us to accept that God loves us unconditionally just as we are and wants to be part of our daily lives? Ashsah, in our story, suffered terrible pain and depression until she let God come into her life. Do you think you might be able to do the same thing? We all want to lead happy and productive lives even though we know that all people must deal with some pain, sorrow or disappointment. How can I shed the pretense of control and turn everything over to God? It isn't easy for us to open our door and let God in...but it is possible. Can you imagine how much joy your life would experience if each human moment was truly shared with God? I wish I could tell you that I have reached that point but, alas, I am still working on that. Nonetheless, let us all strive to unlock the doors of our personal human prisons and ask God to come in and dwell within us. If we can do so, our personal heaven will start right here on earth.

Greg Hadley

ISAAC, A SHEPHERD AT BETHEHEM
Luke 2: 8 – 18

    I'm an old man now, but I have seen some wondrous things during my life. When I was nineteen years old, just beginning to work and fending for myself, I had an experience few other men will ever have. Now, looking back, I understand how profoundly I was affected by this event. That is very important to me because I have spent all these years consigned to the lowest possible class of people in this land. So many others were better educated, performed more important work, acquired a good deal of wealth or had an impact on the social, political or religious life in this country. And yet, it was I, insignificant and lowly, who had a personal encounter with the Messiah, the Son of the Living God. Few others can make that claim. Let me take you back many years and tell you what happened to me and my friends one chilly December night. After you hear my story, you will know why my life was changed in the dark of that winter evening.

    Jobs were very scarce when I was a young man. My father was a day laborer with no social or economic standing in the community. He scarcely made enough money to feed our large family. As the oldest son, I was eager to leave the fairly chaotic situation in our home and strike out on my own. Do not misunderstand: I loved my parents and siblings, but I yearned to be free of the wretched poverty we all experienced every day. From age fourteen, I worked alongside my father, hiring myself out to anyone that needed manual labor. Some days I found work, others I did not. It was a meager existence; what I did earn, I was expected to turn over to our household coffers to help feed and clothe the family.

When I was sixteen, I heard about a farmer who owned a flock of sheep. The farmer's hired shepherd had taken ill, and he was looking for someone else to manage his flock. I was initially reluctant to seek this job. Being a shepherd was considered the lowest of all occupations, reserved for those who were too stupid or lazy to find a respectable job. Sheepherding was considered dirty, smelly work, subject to harsh weather day and night, isolated from most other people and worthy of only minimum pay. This occupation certainly did not warrant a front seat in the synagogue! On the other hand, the work was steady and produced a small but regular wage. After some hesitation, I spoke with the prospective employer who eventually offered me the job. Actually, I did have one important qualification; I liked animals and they seemed to like me. I believed some level of rapport between a shepherd and the sheep would probably help make the job easier.

With only minimum instruction, I began my job. My boss had a number of herds so I was only one of several shepherds he employed. I was sent out to spend three days with an experienced man who half-heartedly told me some of the things I must do and not do. For example, it would be my job to lead the animals to acceptable fields for grazing. I was warned not to poach the areas coveted by the more senior shepherds. They could make my life miserable if I failed to take the grazing areas that were "left over." I was also advised how to construct a sheepfold out of rocks strewn about the land. Finally, I was told how to care for the pregnant animals and their offspring when they were born. Most of the work was common sense and merely required a general sense of responsibility and a basic respect for God's simple creatures.

My flock totaled about one hundred animals, mostly sheep but with a few goats as well. I was surprised by two things. First, each of the animals seemed to have a distinct personality. Some were easy going, happy and relaxed while others were sullen, stubborn and tense. Second, even though they seemed to all look alike, I was able to quickly distinguish one from another. Each seemed to possess a unique mark or physical difference that made them easy to differentiate. I mused that they were distinctive creatures of God, just like human beings. Yes, the job was dirty, smelly and difficult, but I swiftly learned to like the work and quickly became quite attached to my new "friends," the animals. They seemed to like me too.

Most of the shepherds were tending their flocks in adjacent pastures and fields. At the end of the day, many of the men would meet in a common area to share an evening meal and some banal conversation about the events of the day. As with all other groups, there were some of the shepherds I liked better than others, but that is to be expected. The best part of these shared meals was the chance to have human contact that helped to overcome the isolation and loneliness we all faced each day.

Then came that fateful December night I told you about previously. Several of us were gathered in the evening for a light meal. A few young boys had been left to watch over the flocks that were settled for the night. Talk turned to the census called by the Romans that had swelled Bethlehem's population with visitors. There were also comments about the clear nighttime sky and the unusually bright star seen directly overhead. No one recalled seeing that particular star before. Our evening gathering had been made festive because our boss had provided us with a fresh skin full of very good wine. This was a special treat for all the shepherds and each one savored his cup of this pleasant drink. The embers of our fire were glowing red and the wine seemed to be having a relaxing effect. The men seated around the fire suddenly became quiet. At that moment, all the shepherds were startled to see a large man standing near their circle. He was dressed in a flowing white tunic and there was an eerie bright light surrounding him. His presence put a great fear into all of us. Who was he? What did he want of us? Some of the men actually got up and began to run away, but the man gently called them all back to the circle telling them not to be afraid. He informed us that he was bringing very good news of great joy, and not only for us, but for all the people. He proclaimed, today in the city of David a savior has been born for you who is the Messiah and Lord. As the shimmering light around him intensified, he said, you shepherds should go to Bethlehem where you will find an infant wrapped in swaddling clothes and lying in a manger. With that, there was an explosion of color in the sky and the man was suddenly surrounded with a host of beautiful creatures who were singing the most wonderful song I had ever heard: "Glory to God in the highest and on earth peace to those on whom his favor rests." All of us were hypnotized by the event unfolding in front of our eyes. Had we been visited by angels from heaven? Where did all the light come from? What had God just done to us?

As quickly as our angelic visitor had appeared he vanished along with all his friends. The light was gone, the music ended, the clear dark night sky returned and enveloped us. All of us sat there, stunned and shaken by what had occurred and trying to make sense out of it. One of the senior men suggested we should go to Bethlehem as we had been told and seek out the infant who had been declared the Messiah and Lord. No one was able to suggest how we might accomplish this, but all felt compelled to hurry down the hills into the city and try to find the child. What a ragtag bunch we must have appeared as we scampered toward the village.

Where should we begin looking? One man said he knew of a home that rented rooms to visitors. As we approached the place, I looked up and saw that the bright star we had noticed was directly overhead. Why not try here, someone asked? A sleepy innkeeper responded to our persistent knock. Yes, there is a young family here, he told us. They came in late last night and the woman delivered a baby soon thereafter. They are down in the stable; I had to put them there because all my rooms were rented. You will find them at the end of the building where we keep the animals. After a quick thanks to the innkeeper, we hurried the few paces to the manger. There we found a beautiful young woman with her attentive husband caring for a tiny infant. We had all seen babies before and knew they are cute and lovable little bundles of joy...when they are not crying for some kind of attention. The scene we shepherds stumbled upon was different somehow. The couple seemed to exude a special glow and was surrounded with an aura of peacefulness and calm. The infant was different altogether. Just one day old, he was able to focus his eyes on each person in the group and I sensed he understood who we were and what we were doing there. I told the woman about our encounter with the angelic forms up in the hills. She seemed to with serenity accept the story but marveled with us about what had happened. She said her name was Mary, her husband, Joseph. When I told her the angel said this infant was both Messiah and Lord, she offered a tranquil smile and proclaimed softly, I believe that is true. That hit me like a lightning bolt. Was I truly in the presence of the Messiah? Of the Lord God? I looked intently into the child's eyes. He looked back and sweetly curled the corners of his mouth into a lovely smile. I got the feeling he was thinking, thank you for coming to visit me, Isaac; I will hold a special place in my heart for you.

Soon it became obvious that we were overstaying our welcome. Mary and Joseph were tired and the infant was finally becoming fussy. One man had a button in his pocket; he offered it as a gift to the baby. Another carried a small block of cheese that he gave to Joseph. Yet another had gathered a bunch of wildflowers as we came down from the hills and gave them to Mary. They were all humble gifts but given in a spirit of love and admiration. The young couple gratefully accepted these small offerings and sincerely thanked each of us for coming to share in the joy of this new birth.

We all left and returned to our posts. We climbed the hills in silence; no one knew what to say or how to express the feelings we all possessed. The angel told us we would find the Messiah and the Lord. Could it possibly be true? It made no sense to me that the real Messiah would be born in such humble circumstances. Wouldn't an important person such as he be born in a palace somewhere? Instead of being wrapped in cut up rags, shouldn't the Messiah be dressed in the finest clothes available? Why would the Almighty God pick us, lowly shepherds, to encounter the Son of Man in such a way? What were we to do with this information? Would we all be called crazy, or worse, for making up such an unbelievable story? All these things, and more, swirled in my mind as we made it back to our flocks, gently resting for the night. I did not have answers for the many questions churning inside me but I knew one thing for sure, I had been given a once-in-a-lifetime experience that was certain to change every moment of my life ahead.

Allow me to jump forward many years. The time since that nighttime encounter with the Messiah has mostly been filled with humdrum routine. It was over thirty years later that stories began circulating about a prophet named Jesus who was the Messiah according to his disciples. I wondered: could this be the baby I saw, now grown to manhood and beginning his mission? I did believe that long-ago night and was willing to believe again. My work did not permit me time to seek out Jesus to hear him or meet him anew. I was forced to rely on the local gossip about his preaching, cures and miracles throughout the land. I was careful never to boast about my distant encounter with Jesus. Who would believe me anyway?

I saw Jesus one more time, on the Sunday before he was crucified. I was standing on the side of the road as he entered Jerusalem on a donkey. There was a large throng of people but he picked me out as he passed by. Smiling, he said to me, Isaac—it's been a long time! Good to see you again...and then he was gone, surrounded by the crowd. He remembered me! I was thrilled by his greeting. The news about his brutal death greatly saddened me. I wondered how I could have been so wrong about him, thinking he was the Messiah. The Messiah would never die on a cross...would he? Next came the word that Jesus had been raised from the dead and was appearing throughout the land. I was terribly confused by these mixed messages. First, there was death. Now, there was resurrection. What did this mean? Could it possibly be true? No mere human had ever been resurrected. I recalled the angel telling us about the Messiah and Lord. Was this man who knew my name thirty years later the Lord God Almighty? The thought overwhelmed me. Why was I, the most humble of men, allowed to see God made Man twice in my life?

In these final years of my life, I have dedicated myself to learning more about Jesus, his preaching and the human church he left behind him. The number of people who are his disciples is growing very rapidly. I am but one tiny cog in this movement to make Jesus known throughout the world. People need to know that he died for them to open the gates of heaven to all believers. Most of us had no idea this was the work of the Messiah. Now we do.

Think about the concept of faith. Most of us live our lives making frequent acts of faith about many things. You stand on the corner waiting for a bus marked "downtown." When it arrives, you board believing the bus will take you there. You mail a letter across country and expect that it will be delivered. You can feel the breeze on your face but cannot see the air movement. You may believe in God even though you have not seen God. What is faith? It's confidence in some person or thing. It is belief in something that cannot be proved. When we narrow this down to the religious component of our lives, faith—along with hope and love—is a critical element of our spirituality. There are ideas about faith we should always remember. First, our faith in God is a gift, not something we earn or are necessarily entitled to. Like a flower garden, we must figuratively nourish and water our faith or it may wither and die. Second, most people will face occasional doubts that challenge their faith. In our story, Isaac was given information directly by an angel, saw Jesus as an infant, and again at the end of his ministry. In spite of that, Isaac's soul was full of questions and uncertainty. We should learn from this, thanking God for the gift of faith. When we face hesitation and confusion about our faith, we need to pray for greater acceptance and, as scripture says, "help me with my unbelief."

It is also important to understand that this wonderful gift from God is not reserved just for those who are especially wise, holy or steeped with knowledge. Faith is available to all, as our story tells us, "...to the most humble of men."

Greg Hadley

MILCAH, A GIRL BROUGHT TO LIFE
Mark 5: 21 – 24; 35 – 43

My father and mother told me that I had to tell this story. They felt that few people would believe what happened to me unless I was personally willing to share all the details of this extraordinary event. You must forgive me; I'm just twelve years old and probably don't have the skill or vocabulary to tell this story perfectly but I will do my best. I have asked my older brother, Thomas, to help me write this account. While it will be my story, much of it will be Thomas' words. For example, the word *extraordinary* above—I'm not exactly sure what it means, but Thomas told me it was a good word to use in that sentence.

When I was born, my parents knew at once that I was not a completely healthy child. Doctors didn't know much about how to diagnose birth defects so everyone was just guessing what might be wrong with me. I was told that I grew at a slower pace than most children and it was obvious that I had little stamina for running and jumping, you know, all the things kids do when they are two or three years old. I think that made my parents very protective of me as I grew. They shielded me from many activities that would leave me breathless and exhausted. When I was old enough to have a basic understanding that I was "different" from other children, my parents would tell me God had given me a heart with a little broken part in it. That is why I must be careful not to play too hard or try to keep up with other kids because doing so might make me really, really sick. I suppose I was more curious than scared about my condition. It never occurs to someone my age that a child might actually die. Only old people die, I thought. Oh, yes, there was that one incident when a neighbor child had died but he had fallen out of a tree and hit his head on a rock. It was merely an accident, I was told, caused because God suddenly required another angel in heaven and this boy was needed to take that job.

Meanwhile, the hope that I might somehow outgrow my malady faded. By the time I reached ten years of age I was beginning to understand intellectually that I was not well and death for me at any time was a real possibility. That realization made me very interested about the whole idea of life, death, what dying might be like and what happened to you after you actually died. I did not know how to raise these issues with my parents but, on several occasions, I posed some hypothetical (a Thomas word) questions to them. Sometimes children are very good judges of the current situation and I could tell that my queries left both father and mother very uncomfortable.

My father's name is Jairus. He is a senior official in the synagogue, responsible for all the financial matters and the maintenance of the building and grounds. While he is not a rabbi, he performs many important duties and is a highly respected member of the community. Because of his active religious affiliation, I think of my father as my primary teacher about everything related to God and personal spirituality. As his life partner, my mother is also very busy with religious activities and a great source of spiritual direction to our family. But father is such a commanding, powerful figure. I just look to him for answers in the spiritual realm.

Of course, I asked all the questions a kid might pose. Where is heaven? What is it like there? Does it hurt when you die? What is the difference between being alive and being dead? Once you are dead, can you ever come back to life? Why do we immediately bury the body of someone who has died? Does everyone on earth have to die? Why? Sometimes these innocent, childish questions can force adults to examine deeply their own feelings and beliefs about these profound issues. I could tell that my parents, in spite of their substantial education about all things spiritual, really struggled to form simple answers to my questions. As time passed, I did notice that my parents seemed to be more willing to engage me in conversation about the meaning of death and what they thought about a possible afterlife.

During my eleventh year, my condition worsened. With only mild exertion, I would often become dizzy followed by unconsciousness. When this happened, I would get the feeling that I was being squeezed into a funnel-shaped gray tunnel that was totally dark at the far end. When everything was completely black, I experienced a noise as if my head were under water hearing a dull, metallic gurgling sound. When I regained consciousness, I was often disoriented for several moments and had trouble focusing my eyes. After each one of these episodes I felt utterly exhausted and found it difficult to get up out of my bed. Without saying a word, I could tell that my parents were deeply worried about me. Probably their greatest frustration centered on the fact there was nothing to do to help me. Following one of these fainting events, I asked my father if I will know when I have died. Tears welled up in his eyes. My dearest daughter, he whispered, I believe in my heart that you will come face to face with Almighty God when you die, and he will lead you by the hand to paradise. But I don't know that for sure. No one has ever died and then returned to explain how things happen. But my faith tells me that God is gentle and merciful to all of us when the time comes. And, surely, there is a final moment for each of us including you, me, your mother and everyone on earth. Dear Milcah, I hope your time is a long way off. But, we must put that in God's hands because none of us know or control the time of our death. He leaned down, took my face in his hands and placed a gentle kiss on my forehead. I had made my Abba so sad, and I was sorry for that.

Even youngsters can sense when their bodies are starting to shut down in anticipation of death. I cannot explain to you the exact feeling, but I just *knew* that the end of my life was fast approaching. There were some obvious signs like a dramatic reduction of my appetite, less intake of fluids, a darkening of my urine and frequent periods of semi-consciousness. I sensed that nearby relatives and friends were visiting me frequently, standing around my bed and speaking in hushed voices. Even I could recognize this was the beginning of a deathwatch.

Because of my father's prominence in the Jewish religious community, he knew and had met Jesus of Nazareth, the latest prophet. It was common knowledge, even among those who felt threatened by Jesus, that the young rabbi had done many cures and miracles and seemed to be truly blessed by the Almighty God. I overheard my father tell my mother that he intended to approach Jesus and ask him to come to our home to lay hands on me to cure my malady. A few days later, I again heard a conversation between mother and father. Soon thereafter, father departed to find Jesus and ask for his help. I learned much later that my father found Jesus and fell prostrate before him begging Jesus to come to our home and cure me so that I would get well and live a happy life.

Soon after my father left to find the prophet, I had the strong feeling that I was entering the final stage of my earthly life. I drifted in and out of consciousness still experiencing the aural sense of dark funnels, being underwater and blackness. Then, suddenly I found myself enveloped in a totally different dream state. I was walking in a long, large tube or tunnel. It was brilliantly lighted, but I could not see where the tunnel ended. As I walked along I began to see an indistinct figure up ahead. The figure was extending a hand to me, but I was never able to get close enough to grasp it. The further I walked into the tunnel, the brighter the light seemed. I felt I was seeing sparkling red, gold and blue shimmers of light on the walls of the tunnel. While this was occurring, I could barely hear my mother saying in a passionate voice, O, Milcah, my darling girl, don't leave me! Shortly after hearing my mother, the light I was seeing began to fade, the tunnel seemed to collapse around me and everything became pitch black. I am doing my best to describe what I felt happening. I have absolutely no idea what any of this means. I sensed that I was in the total darkness for a period of time, but I don't know how long.

    My next remembrance is hearing a soft, gentle voice of a man saying in Hebrew, *talitha koum*, which means, little girl, I say to you arise. After a moment, I opened my eyes. Even in the darkened room, I immediately saw my mother and father. They both had looks of shocked disbelief on their faces. I also saw four other men standing around my bed. The one closest to me was very handsome and had a beautiful smile. He was holding my hand. The other three men appeared much like my parents with startled but joyful expressions on their rugged young faces. The man near me said, Milcah, I am Jesus. Your parents and all your friends and neighbors have been very sad because they thought you had died. I came to see you since I knew you were just sleeping. Come, Milcah, get up. Your parents are going to prepare some food for you to eat. You must be very hungry after your long sleep. Then Jesus turned to his friends and my parents and said, the people get excited when they hear about events like this. It is unfortunate that their enthusiasm is often generated for the wrong reason. Many of them are looking for a magical way to throw off the yoke of the Romans and they view this type of cure as another proof that I may be the magician they have waited for. That is not what my mission is about. Therefore, I ask all of you not to discuss with others what I have done to wake Milcah. The most important thing is that she is awake and restored to good health. That is enough to make all of us in this room happy.

When father had traveled to find Jesus, he begged the young prophet to come to our home and cure me, his little girl. Jesus said yes but was delayed by the very large crowd and several others who begged for his help. Just as Jesus and my father were heading toward our town, one of our neighbors arrived and told my dad that I was already dead. Father was devastated by this news, but Jesus said to him, do not be afraid; just have faith. Jesus then set out to find me. He took along three of his disciples named Peter, James and John. When they arrived at our home, all of our relatives and neighbors had assembled and were beginning the traditional Jewish Mourner's Kaddish, or service for the dead including the baleful wailing and crying for the one who had passed away. Jesus asked those gathered what was going on and they told him I was dead. Jesus said to them you are mistaken. Milcah is not dead; she is merely asleep. Many of the mourners ridiculed Jesus telling him he was a fool and worse. Gently but firmly, Jesus asked all the mourners to leave the house, permitting only mother and father and his three friends to stay with him. The rest of the story I have already told you.

When Jesus woke me, it was the first and only time I ever saw him. I wonder: did he bring me back to life or was I merely sleeping very soundly as he said? I probably will not know the answer to that until that final day when I do finally step across the threshold from life into death. Perhaps then some of my questions will be answered.

Father and mother were transformed by Jesus' visit and what he did for me. They spoke to me earnestly about what I had experienced while I lay in my bed apparently dead, according to those who checked on me. I did my best to convey what I remembered about the tunnel, the lights, the indistinct figure that I could not quite reach. Each new day dulled my memory. After a couple of weeks,

I hardly remembered anything. I was so joyful to finally be well and able to run and dance and sing with my playmates. That one thing I will never forget: Jesus made me well. I am forever grateful.

Milcah's remarkable story speaks about hope and the recognition that God will intervene in our lives to help us work through difficult situations. I did not say that God would personally fix everything that is wrong, but that he will never give us anything that we can't handle with his help. Jairus never gave up hoping that a saving treatment could be found for his daughter. He tried everything he could, even turning to a young prophet with unknown credentials for a potential cure. Consider how difficult life would become if we didn't have the virtue of hope. Hope convinces us that there is a solution to every intractable circumstance we might face. Milcah herself was probably too young to have a strong impression about hope. But she counted on her parents to maintain a firm sense of hope for her ultimate cure and return to complete health. This young lady was able to rely on Jesus for a final solution to her life-threatening situation.

This story also tests our belief about death. Intellectually, every adult knows all human life eventually comes to an end. In spite of accepting this abstract notion, most of us believe that the end of our own life is on a far and indistinct horizon. Yes, I know the end is out there somewhere but I also think there is plenty of time left to me. Of course, the diagnosis of stage four terminal cancer in one of the vital organs can be a wake-up call for anyone of us. It is then we begin to answer the innocent questions that Milcah posed to her parents. Yes, what will the afterlife be like...if there is an afterlife? Is there a place called heaven? Or hell? What actually happens to me when I breathe my last breath? Those of us with Christian beliefs and education can sometimes recite the Catechism answers about eternal life. Like Milcah's father, we know the answers but are not sure how everything actually works out. Which brings us back to hope. Each of us prays that we will cooperate with God's graces as we try to live out a Christian life taught to us in sacred scripture and the teachings of the Church. We are also full of hope that, when we meet God face to face at the end of our human life, he will be merciful, gentle and forgiving for the many times we have succumbed to human weakness and frailty. I personally hope the God who casts final judgment on me is more merciful than he is just.

Greg Hadley

BARUCH – THE WINE STEWARD AT CANA
John 2: 2 – 11

    As a young boy of thirteen I began to assist my father in his business. He supplied food, drink and staff for weddings and other celebrations especially for the well-to-do citizens in the region. Father offered many options to his customers including very simple food and drink to lavish meals with the choicest wines. Our reputation was excellent; when my father was hired to do a job, everyone knew things would be close to perfect. Father would hire people in the community to help him prepare the food. He also had a group of regular workers who would provide every aspect of service including setting up all the tables and tents, transporting the food to the site, serving of the food and wine to the guests and the cleanup after the event was over. We had a large inventory of kiln-fired plates and goblets, tables and chairs, beautiful cloth dressings for the tables and impressive serving dishes for food. Even as a youngster, I remember being in awe of all the things my father had accumulated to operate his business.

    As time went on, father bought a small vineyard, grew grapes and processed the fruit into his own wine each year. The vineyard contained two varieties of grapes so he was able to produce several delicious wines. As I grew to manhood, father put me in charge of the vines and the wine producing operation. Of utmost importance, father said, was that the wine, or *yayin* in Hebrew, be produced in strict compliance with Jewish dietary laws. In other words, the wine must be *mevushal* or Kosher. That made perfect sense because the great majority of our customers were observant Jews who would insist on Kosher at their banquets and festivals.

Although we didn't know exactly how the wine making process worked or what caused the wine to ferment, we learned by trial and error how to produce excellent wine. The grapes matured on the vines during the hot and dry days of summer. As autumn approached, we checked the grapes daily for water content, plumpness and sweetness. It was always a guess about when to pick the fruit; but once the process began, it was necessary to complete the harvest very quickly. Over-plump and sugary grapes would rot very quickly.

There was an abundance of limestone rock on the land. We used this material to fashion our wine presses, called *gat* in Hebrew. At harvest, the grapes would be put into the presses and crushed so that what remained were the grape juice and the skins. The presses were always placed on elevated ground so that gravity would direct the juice and skins through a stone canal to a lower fermenting pit. Here an undefined natural process occurs where the juice apparently has interaction with yeast on the skins. This produces alcohol in the juice turning it into wine. We could not precisely measure the alcohol content of the wine. With experience we learned when to stop the fermenting process so that we had a "good wine," in Greek *kalon oinon*, that had the proper level of alcohol content. When the fermentation was complete, the mixture was thoroughly strained and the wine was transferred to storage devices. The properly fermented wine could now be stored for a long period without spoiling. We normally introduced a new vintage of wine to our customers and friends at *Sukkot*, also known as The Feast of Tabernacles, which celebrated the fall harvest of the fields including grapes.

The storage of the final wine product was a very delicate matter. There were four major ways we could store the wine. Most common was the wine skin made from animal hides. This was an effective and relatively inexpensive method; but if the fermentation process continued, we might wind up with a ruptured skin and lose a good deal of wine. Second, we stored some wine in large jugs handmade of clay and fired to hardness. Again, this method was inexpensive but any rough handling could break the jugs resulting in lost wine. Stone jars proved to be good storage devices although they were very heavy and often difficult to move. Finally, during the last several decades, many craftsman located around the Mediterranean Sea had learned to heat sand and combine it with several chemicals to form a substance called glass. This new product could be shaped into small containers, called bottles, which proved to be very effective storage units for our wine although somewhat expensive. We felt it necessary to continually stay abreast of the latest new innovations in order to remain competitive in our business. Studying new methods of wine making and implementing them into our operations was the part of my work I found most personally satisfying.

My father taught me that making good wine was God's work. He often quoted from Psalm 104, Verses 14 and 15, which say, in part:

> *You bring bread from the earth,*
> *and wine to gladden our hearts.*

While father believed wine making was noble, there were members of society who voiced great concern about potential negative effects of alcohol and the problems of excessive drinking. It was true that some abused alcohol to the detriment of their family and community, but father felt these were mostly rare exceptions. In his view, and mine, wine was a delightful gift from God that added pleasure to many people's lives.

Our society offered a real dichotomy. There was a class of businessmen, merchants, storekeepers, political and religious leaders who often possessed great wealth. Conversely, many in the community were quite poor and were required to scratch out a living for themselves and their families. My father and his family worked hard and, while we were not wealthy, we were certainly well off materially. Father preached generosity to all of us, and we did our part to help the needy. In addition, he hired many in the community so they did share in the fruits of our business to some extent. I felt a sense of empathy for the poor but no guilt for my family's success, either. We worked diligently and my father had to take many risks to grow the business. Yet, the issue of rich and poor was often a central theme of my thought process. How could the rich help more people to rise up from poverty to create better lives for their families? What kind of self-motivation was necessary for the poor to seek opportunities in small business ventures? It was not easy for me to easily discern a solution to these problems.

    A very influential wine merchant in Cana was planning a marriage feast for his daughter. He contacted my father about providing all the arrangements for the event with the exception that the merchant planned to serve his own wine not ours. Father was disappointed since much of our profit was generated by the sale of our wine. However, the party was to be very large so a substantial catering fee was available. Father asked me to be the chief steward for this job, which meant my responsibilities would be significant. I enjoyed being in charge so I looked forward to the occasion. I traveled to Cana three days before the party to make sure all the arrangements were in order. The guest list was very diverse. It included the elite members of society but also many common folk. The wine merchant's assistant pointed out to me the name Jesus of Nazareth on the list. I was told that Jesus was a very popular young preacher in the region. A number of his disciples had also been invited to the wedding along with his mother. I had not heard of this Jesus before so I was interested in the story but soon forgot about it as other issues occupied my time and attention. One item I considered to be a serious problem. In my opinion, the wine merchant had underestimated the consumption of wine by his guests. I pointed out to him that I was worried about the supply but he dismissed my concern as excessive anxiety by a young man. I've been dealing with wine my entire adult life, he told me. I think I would know how much wine my guests will require. Yes, I thought, he has more than twice the experience that I have. Still, as the day of the feast arrived, I was uneasy about the wine supply.

The host was very pleased with the arrangements for his daughter's wedding feast. The day was lovely and warm (but not too hot) and the food we had prepared was plentiful and delicious. We had adequate service staff to take care of guests' needs so I spent most of my time mingling with the people attending the event to insure they were enjoying the food and that all requests were satisfied. I met Jesus, several of his friends and his mother during the day. He was a center of attention with many gathered around him. His contact with others appeared to be easy and warm. He looked relaxed and happy and kept a constant smile on his face. When I spoke to him, he complimented me for the wonderful food. My friends and I don't often eat this well and I'm enjoying every bite, he said. His young disciples were all ruggedly handsome although rough-hewn men but very polite and quite deferent to Jesus. His mother was a truly lovely woman, very kind and gentle to all who approached her. I was very impressed with her overall demeanor and gracefulness. Jesus was very attentive to her and they often engaged in brief conversation.

About two hours into the event, I went to the kitchen area to check on supplies of food and wine. Everything related to food was fine but my worry about the wine supply appeared justified. We were reduced to just a couple of small jugs of wine and the party was in full swing. The host approached me, very chagrined, admitting he had failed to properly provide for the wine

Jesus Face-To-Face

needs. Frantically he said, I will be disgraced by this mistake! Just at that moment, a group of serving staff carried in six stone water jars brimming with liquid. What is this all about, I wondered? My wine supervisor, Aaron, then took a small cup, dipped into one of the jars and held out the cup for me to sample. It was the most delicious wine I had ever tasted. Looking into the stone jars, I saw they were all filled to the brim with this wine, at least one hundred twenty gallons in all. Seeking out the host, I said to him, everyone serves the best wine first, and then when people have drunk freely, an inferior wine is served. Apparently you have saved the very best of your wine until now. He looked at me dumbfounded and said nothing in reply. The staff busied themselves readying the wine for distribution to the guests. I called the supervisor over and asked him if he knew what had happened. Yes, Baruch, I do know, he said, and I cannot believe what I have just witnessed.

According to Aaron, Mary, the mother of Jesus, observed that the supply of wine for the guests had run very low. Mary then said to Jesus, they have no more wine to serve their guests. Aaron told me that Jesus looked slightly annoyed by Mary's comment and said to her, Woman, how does this concern of yours affect me? Aaron then said Jesus followed up with a comment, "My hour has not yet come". Both Aaron and I wondered what Jesus meant by that. Mary ignored Jesus' mild pique and turned to the staff saying, do whatever Jesus tells you. Aaron then told me Jesus directed that six of the stone ceremonial washing jars be filled to the top with water. After this, Jesus requested that some of the water be drawn out and given to the chief steward. Now, Aaron said, you know as much as I do Baruch. What I witnessed a few moments before as jars full of water had suddenly become premium wine. How did that happen, Aaron asked? I had no idea, of course, and felt as befuddled and amazed as Aaron.

Towards the end of the day as the guests were departing, I found Jesus thanking the host for the wonderful and festive party. As Jesus slowly walked toward the front gate of the home, I said to him, can you help me understand what happened with the wine in the six stone jars? He paused and looked at me with a slight smile. Baruch, he said, I have been given an important mission to fulfill. I am just now embarking on this work my father sent me to accomplish. My mother pointed out to me that a friend needed help and I provided the assistance that she requested of me. It turns out that you saw the first sign of my work and who I am. I hope you have further opportunities to find out everything about me, Jesus said. He extended his hand to shake mine then turned and departed. I never saw Jesus of Nazareth again.

As the years passed, I heard a great deal more about Jesus—his life, a gruesome death, resurrection from the dead and a growing company of believers long after he left this earth. I consider myself to be greatly blessed by having witnessed one of Jesus' earliest miracles. Through deep reflection and prayer, I came to believe that Jesus was the Christ, the Son of God, a savior sent by his Father to open the gates of heaven for all believers. I am one of the luckiest men alive to have met and known the Messiah who was fully man and fully God.

The story about Baruch and the wedding feast of Cana provides three ideas to think about.

First, we hear of an over confident host who is quite sure of himself but winds up making a big mistake about the amount of wine necessary to satisfy his guests. How often do you and I make a similar error about our own abilities, especially our spiritual strengths? We charge ahead in life without a humble reliance on God for the help we need to live our lives in accordance with the gospel message? So many of us become full of ourselves, and think we reach spiritual goals without help from God. How wrongheaded that idea turns out to be. It's hard to say help me Lord, I can't do this on my own. But that is what we need to plead for.

Second, this story provides a wonderful example of honor to one's parents. Jesus was not planning on performing his first sign when he went to the wedding. Mary saw a need and asked her son to help. After a natural moment of human hesitation, he did what his mother asked of him. Those of us with aging parents or grandparents need to be continually reminded that respect, care and love are duties we owe to our elders.

Finally, we see a biblical example of the haves and have-nots in society. Today they are referred to as the 1% and the 99%. Often this devolves into class warfare where the 99% are envious of the rich and demand equality of outcomes instead of equality of opportunity. They wish to play a "zero sum" game of taking from the rich so they can have more...with no additional effort. For their part the 1% often disdain all the rest and fail to pay heed to the biblical call "to whom much has been given, much will be expected." If you are part of the 99%, try through hard work and ambition to find a way to a better life. If part of the 1%, never forget your need to be generous to those less fortunate than you are.

Greg Hadley

SARAI – THE POOR WIDOW
Mark 12: 41-44

I cannot think of anyone who has led a more obscure and undistinguished life than I have. I am not ashamed of this nor am I complaining. It just turns out that I wasn't blessed with many personal gifts so I had little opportunity to do important things. I was fortunate to have friends—many of them—and when I was married I was a loving and dutiful wife. My husband and I shared a deep spiritual belief in Almighty God and we did our best to lead the lives of observant Jews. We set aside some time daily for personal prayer, attended temple on the Sabbath and celebrated all the major holy days as best we could.

It is probably true that my husband and I gravitated to each other because of the similarities in our personalities. We were both quiet and reserved by nature. Neither of us would have ever thought to be outgoing or animated in our relations with other people. I guess we were more comfortable always being in the background in any situation. One could fairly say that we were the perfect definition of dull people.

My husband and I loved each other and we both worked hard at being caring and considerate of one another. I do have a deep regret about the years we were married; God did not bless our union with any children. I am sorry about that since my husband would have been a good father and I think I would have been a good mother.

Our lack of social aggressiveness probably affected our financial situation as well. My husband always seemed to be the last man selected when there was work to be done. That meant we often had the bare minimum to eat. Our clothes were clean but worn and our shelter was very modest. Again, I want you to understand that I am not complaining about this. God blessed us in many other ways and we daily gave thanks for what we did have. Even though our income was meager, we always tried to save some small amount to contribute to the temple treasury when we attended services. Often the amount was embarrassingly small, but I felt that God knew we were doing what we could. It was a little hurtful when we saw the look of disdain on the faces of others in the temple when we made our weekly contribution. Frankly, some weeks we had nothing to contribute and that made us feel uneasy.

In spite of the material hardship we faced, our lives were happy and we were glad to have each other. Things changed one day when my husband arrived home from work exhausted and dizzy. I thought that he may have just experienced a particularly strenuous day and a good night's rest would restore him. That was not the case. The next morning he was still very unsteady and was now having some difficulty breathing. I summoned help from a physician in the neighborhood but that failed to revive him. By the end of the day, my husband had died. The doctor told me that the cause of death was probably a complete failure of the heart. I was deeply saddened by this loss but accepted that God's will had been done so I must learn to live with changed circumstances.

During my married life, I learned to be quite a good cook and baker. I was especially successful in putting together "something from nothing." One of my creations best liked by my husband was a small cake made with dried grapes and honey. They were easy to make but very tasty. I decided I would bake these cakes in large batches and sell them in the neighborhood to earn my livelihood now that my spouse was gone. This provided a small but steady source of income. I was grateful for that.

Rabbi Jesus of Nazareth had been speaking in our temple precincts recently. Although his message often seemed radical to conservative Jews, he was quite popular and seemed to have a large group of followers. Seldom has the elite religious and political class been so roundly criticized by an itinerant preacher like Jesus. He infuriated the scribes and Pharisees by pointing out their hypocrisy with very direct language. Jesus also appeared to have an agile mind and was never trapped by the ambiguous questions and comments directed toward him. When I had the opportunity, I always enjoyed listening to Jesus, but I worried that he was creating some very deep-seated animosity with many influential people in the society. I believed that could cause Jesus a serious problem someday.

Jesus was present at one of our Sabbath services. When the time came, the treasury purse was passed throughout the congregation. Some of the wealthy members made a big show of placing a large amount of money into the purse. When it was finally my turn, I put in two small coins, each having very little value. I had learned by this time not to be embarrassed by the size of my offering; God knew what was in my heart. When it was time for Jesus to preach, he spoke about the fact that everything we have in life—everything—is a gift from God. Since all we have has been freely given to us we, too, should give to those who are less fortunate. Jesus then commented on how generous many of the wealthy temple members had been when they put money in the temple purse. I observed several of these rich people smiling broadly when Jesus complimented them as they glanced knowingly at their friends in the front row of the temple. Just as quickly, Jesus then said these large gifts had little meaning since the donations had been contributed from surplus wealth. Looking directly at me, Jesus said, this poor widow has put more into the treasury than all these rich people in the front row. She has donated from her poverty just about all she had and from her need for livelihood. Jesus concluded, this woman's gift is more valuable than any other given today. The smiles in the front row turned to angry scowls. Once again, Jesus had put down those who boasted about their importance. As for me, my face was flushed as I was singled out for my tiny gift. I felt that every pair of eyes in the temple was focused on me. This made me feel very uncomfortable.

As the service ended, Jesus immediately came to where I was sitting and sat down next to me. Sarai, he said, I hope I did not cause you too much discomfort. I was so impressed with your generosity and felt the need to teach all the others about the proper way to deal with gifts freely given to us by God. Your understanding of the blessings given to you is most pleasing to my Father in heaven. I call down his blessings on you, Sarai, and pray that you will continue to be a gracious source of aid to others. While the amount of your gifts may be small, they come from an enormous heart and soul. God will surely bless you for your generosity, Sarai. Jesus gently put his arm around my shoulder and gave me a hug and a big smile. I was touched by his kindness and care about my feelings. As he left me, Jesus said to me, Sarai, I hope you will continue to listen to my preaching and encourage your friends to do so as well. You are living a beautiful and balanced life now. Please pray for me and my work.

I am now almost forty years old. I think this encounter with Jesus in the temple was the most significant event of my life. Just as he asked, I have tried hard to live by his message of faith, hope and love for God and my neighbor. Have I been a positive influence on others? Well, I don't know that for sure, but I have tried and I believe God knows what is in my heart.

Unfortunately, many of us live our lives punctuated by "if only" or "what if." We wonder how things would have turned out if only we had been richer, better looking, married to a different spouse or employed by a different company. What if we had gone to a different school, lived in another area, invested our savings more aggressively or taken some additional business risks. It is often hard to accept our circumstances as they are and make the best of them. Instead of thanking God for the blessings we do have, we complain that bad luck and poor timing are the real reasons we are not more successful in life. This kind of thinking leads to perpetual unhappiness since we are never satisfied with our state in life no matter what it is. Sarai teaches us that even minimum gifts well used can lead to a successful life. Instead of being envious of what others have, let's all try to be thankful for the gifts we do have and make the most of them.

HELENA, THE SYROPHOENICIAN WOMAN
Mark 7: 25 – 30
Matthew 15: 21 – 28

The most remarkable aspects of my encounter with the prophet Jesus are that I am a woman and I am a Gentile. Either one would normally prevent me from speaking with Jesus or asking him for help. As it turns out, I did both of those things, which resulted in a miraculous outcome for my daughter Melaina. Let me give you some background that will provide context and show you how my meeting with Jesus took place.

I have always lived in and around the Gentile cities of Tyre and Sidon. Both of these cities are ports located on the Mediterranean Sea. My husband, Dimitros, and I have our home just north of Tyre on the banks of the Litani River, which flows from headwaters well north of Damascus into the Sea. Both of us have a Greek heritage. We are called Syrophoenicians because we live in the Greek enclave of Phoenicia that is controlled by Syria. We have just one daughter and she has been the light of our lives. Dimitros is a prosperous olive oil merchant and travels extensively throughout the eastern Mediterranean area selling his products. I do not think of ourselves as wealthy, but we do not lack for material things.

When our daughter was born, we were very happy. We hoped for more children but that did not happen so we doted on Melaina. She seemed to be a normal child who grew physically, intellectually and emotionally in line with other children her age. When she reached her teenage years, she became especially difficult to deal with. I believed she just had an overdose of the hormones all young girls experience as they proceed through puberty. My mother had told me how impossible I was at that same time in my life. I suspected the gods were getting revenge for what I had done to my mother during my teenage years.

I became concerned when Melaina's dark moods and violent outbursts grew more intense instead of subsiding. She would become hysterical over the smallest little thing and rage with wild anger. I even worried for my own safety because she would lash out physically against both me and my husband. Her actions went far beyond the normal reaction to parental control or over-active hormones in a young girl's body. Her conduct was increasingly tempestuous and unmanageable. Even her physical appearance became brutish and ferocious. Dimitros and I were extremely worried about Melaina. We went to every physician in the area seeking some kind of a diagnosis. No help was forthcoming. Finally we were forced to hire a large, strong woman who moved into our home and acted as a keeper for Melaina. Using various drugs and medicines prescribed by the physicians our daughter was kept sedated in a darkened room most of the time and was overseen by the woman keeper. It was a horrible situation, but we did not know what else to do. We were frightened that Melaina might actually do physical harm to herself or to us. We were desperate to find a solution to this monstrous problem.

Neither my husband nor I could be described as religious. We had both been raised in typical Greek homes where there was a casual deference to the pantheon of gods. What little interest there was related to feasts or celebrations to various gods that resulted in good food or elaborate celebrations and parties. I don't remember any real focus on a deep religious or spiritual life. I believed that the gods served mostly as lucky charms or represented bad karma when things were going poorly in life. I think I was counseled to be more superstitious than religious. Sadly, we raised Melaina the same way so she was also void of any spiritual grounding.

Facing the terrible problem we did with our daughter, it would have been better if all of us had some type of spiritual or religious anchor. Alas, that was not to be. I did not know which way to turn.

During a trip to Capernaum in Galilee, my husband saw a Jewish prophet named Jesus of Nazareth. It was coincidence that my husband conducted a business meeting near where Jesus was preaching to his followers. When the meeting concluded, Dimitros heard Jesus speaking. Upon returning to our Tyre home, my spouse told me about this man and his intriguing story. I was informed that Jesus was being credited with many cures and had performed some miracles in his short public life to date. With no religious context, people like us tend to be quite skeptical about such stories. Some of Dimitros' Jewish business associates claimed that Jesus could be the messianic savior of the Jews, the one who would restore the glory of Israel in both a political and religious sense. That sounded like delusional wishful thinking to me. As far as I could see, the Romans were firmly in control of the whole area. I wondered how big an army this Jesus was assembling. He would need a powerful array of troops to defeat the Romans, it seemed to me. I put all this talk of Jesus out of my mind. Of what importance could it possibly be to me?

Meanwhile the condition of my daughter was growing more serious each day. Dimitros and I were frantic to find a solution. Melaina's violent rages were now occurring almost continually. She was not eating properly or getting adequate rest. Her physical deterioration was becoming as critical as her mental state. A local Greek religious leader offered the thought that Melaina might be possessed by an evil spirit. At first I scoffed at the idea and totally rejected the concept. However, the more I pondered this thought, the more plausible it sounded to me. How—or why—a demonic spirit would take over my daughter's spirit, I had no idea. If the possession was actually true, how would we possibly rid Melaina of such an evil being? My mind raced as I tried to sort out all the conflicting points of view.

Just then, Dimitros told me that the Jewish prophet Jesus was planning a trip to our region. As far as we knew, he had never wandered into Gentile territory before. I wondered why he would come here since I had been told his mission was to the people of Israel. There were very few Jews here. Why come to this place? Perhaps he wanted to see how his spiritual message would resonate with Gentiles. While I put little stock in miracle cures, I did want to seek advice about demonic spirits and how they were expelled from a person. Jesus might know, so I decided to seek him out while he was in our area.

It was not easy to track Jesus down. He did not visit close to our home so I had to travel a long distance to find him. He was walking along a road heading back toward Galilee. He was surrounded by his disciples and friends, and they were all chatting as they proceeded down the road. One of the things Dimitros had learned was that Jesus was from the lineage of the great King David of Israel. This was apparently an important fact since Jewish scripture claimed the Messiah would be from the House of David. As I hurried along the road trying to catch up with Jesus, I called out to him, have pity on me, Jesus, son of David! My daughter is tormented by a demon. You must help me! Jesus acted as if he had not heard me and continued walking while speaking with his friends. I continued to cry out, son of David, help me! One of his disciples turned to me and said, be quiet woman! Can't you see that the master is busy? Stop bothering him. As I cried out one more time for his help, Jesus finally paused, turned towards me and said, why do you ask for my help? I was sent only to the lost sheep of the house of Israel. I have no connection to you, a Gentile woman. I was emboldened by my own desperation, and ran up to him prostrating myself in front of where he stood. I pleaded once more, please, Jesus, help my daughter. He paused for a moment, looking at me intently while I was on my knees before him. Then he said to me in a flat, matter-of-fact voice, woman it is not right to take the food intended for the children and give it to the dogs. He was obviously using a metaphor to tell me that his message and his mission were directed to the people of Israel and not to the Gentiles. My mind raced for a reply to his words. I blurted out in my sobbing voice, please, Lord, even the dogs are permitted to eat the scraps that fall off the table of their master. I hoped that my clever reply that turned his own words back onto him would gain his attention. Jesus again became silent and looked at me for several seconds. His face and eyes told me that he was carefully considering what I had just said to him. Finally, he said to me, woman, you seem to have a very great faith. Because of that I am granting your request. Return home now. Your daughter is cured of her malady. Smiling at me, he leaned down and gently touched my cheek then turned and resumed walking down the road.

 I was left there speechless on the dusty road. My heart was bursting with hope and excitement. I sensed I had not encountered a normal man just now. Jesus had an indefinable aura that marked him as someone powerful, transcendent and transformational. I stayed where I was for a few moments gaining my composure and catching my breath. Then I began the hurried trek back to my home hoping to see the miraculous effect of the promise Jesus made to me along the desert road.

 It was several hours before I arrived home in the early evening. I was emotionally drained and physically exhausted as I reached the front door of our home. I felt great anxiety as I entered. What if nothing had changed? My last hope would be shattered. What would I find when I entered Melaina's room? My whole body was shaking as

I reached for the handle. Slowly entering the room, I saw that the curtains had been opened. The keeper was sitting quietly by Melaina's bed, holding my daughter's hand. Hardly able to speak, I said, what is going on? The keeper looked at me. Her face, normally gray and grim, was glowing. She said to me, your daughter suddenly became very peaceful about four hours ago. She sat up in bed, told me she was hungry and thirsty so I prepared something for her to eat and drink. After this light meal, she and I had an extended and wonderful conversation. Melaina was completely different; no more screaming or flailing about. She seemed composed, happy and full of life. I have no idea what caused this profound change but I do know it is a good thing. She seems to be enjoying a deep rest now. Would you like to sit with her, Madam, while I fix myself something to eat? Dazed, I mumbled a quiet, thank you, yes. What had happened, I thought? Could the words of a man fifteen miles distant cause my daughter to be cured? Was she possessed by a demonic spirit? If so, where has the demon gone? My mind swirled with questions to which I found no answers—except for one. Jesus had saved my little girl, of that I had no doubt. What kind of a man was he? How could he be invested with such God-like power to cure other people? The more I thought about my brief encounter with Jesus, the more humble I became. He was not a human being like me, I concluded. No, he was much more than that. How was I ever going to find out exactly who he is? I could not imagine how that would happen.

Dimitros, Melaina and I became delightfully reacquainted in the next few months. It was as if she had been on a long trip and just returned to share the stories of her adventure. Thankfully, she had little remembrance of the difficult times and they quickly faded for my husband and me too. Even with no religious background, I had learned to offer a daily prayer of thanksgiving for Melaina's cure. Not knowing a personal God, I prayed to the one that Jesus loves. I found it incredible that a brief meeting with this son of David could have such a profound influence on my life. I will always be grateful for those few minutes I spent with Jesus.

One of the virtues we try to instill in our children is that of "stick-to-it-ivness" or perseverance. Society in general admires people who never give up and keep plodding forward towards their goals and objectives no matter what. Folks find little merit in those who give up at the first sign of an obstacle or difficulty whether it is in sports, academics or any challenge in life. A Little Leaguer may strike out three times but battles for the base hit in the final inning that knocks in the winning run. The high school freshman struggles with algebra but keeps studying hard and winds up with an A- on the final report card. The young flute player just can't seem to get the finger movements right but perseveres at practice and gets a standing ovation at the spring recital. It's not just kids, either. The virtue of perseverance applies to adults too. We continue to work on improving our skills needed in the business world. We remain steadfast about fundamental issues of good and evil in the face of societal pressures to buckle. We remain faithful to our prayer life even when we feel arid. As the old saying goes, the race is won by slow and steady. In our story, Helena was tempted to give up many times but she continued seeking ways to cure her daughter. Even Jesus initially discouraged her but she didn't give up. Her perseverance resulted in her daughter's cure. Her example serves as a good model for each of us. When we become discouraged and feel ready to throw in the towel, remember the story of Helena.

Greg Hadley

BARTIMAEUS, THE BLIND BEGGAR
Matthew 20: 29 – 34
Mark 10: 35 – 43
Luke 18: 35 – 43

Many who tell their stories about meeting Jesus have much to say. Their lives and how they finally encountered the Son of David make for interesting stories. I wish I could tell you that I had done significant things, came from an unusual home life or experienced some kind of deep spiritual awakening before I had my chance to speak to Jesus. No, I am merely a poor human sent into this world with a tragic flaw—blindness. If you are not blind I presume you will have a difficult time understanding what it truly means to live your life sightless. I have *heard* about the color of the sky, the profile of a large tree, what a full moon looks like on a dark night, but I have no mental picture of what my eyes would truly see. Can you possibly grasp how your life might be limited if you were blind? Think of all the things that would be impossible for you to accomplish without sight. Simple things like walking down a road, protecting one's self from a wild animal, seeing a storm approaching in the sky or merely finding a cup to get a sip of cool water—tasks that are often impossible for the blind without help from another person. Over the years I have learned that whining about my condition does no good, but I had to get that off my chest. To me, blindness equals misery.

As a youngster, you don't really understand what is happening until you begin to have an idea about your environment and who you are. I guess I was about five years old when I began realizing what it meant to be totally blind. I did not see shapes or shadows or very bright light such as the sun. I saw nothing. I had no experience of the world through my eyes. Perhaps that sharpened the input I got from touch, taste, sound and smell, but I got nothing from my sense of sight. I could not go to school because I could not learn to read. Writing would have been impossible too. I was of little help around the house. I could not assist my father Timaeus with his work. I could not play with other children. To my great sorrow I learned that I was essentially helpless physically and virtually hopeless spiritually and emotionally. I often wondered: why had God bothered to create a useless person like me?

    Ah, finally I found something I could do—beg. Even as a teenage boy I would work myself to a spot near the temple. There, I would call out plaintively to those passing by or going to pray asking for small coins to be placed in the fragment of a tattered blanket on the ground in front of me. Some days I would return home in the evening with a small handful of money. Other days there would be nothing. At least I was able to give a pittance to my parents for my keep. They professed their gratefulness, but I always felt humiliated about the way I obtained what little money I did have. Over time I became quite cynical about my "profession." I began rationalizing about the important role I played for the rich people walking on the road. At least some of them could salve their consciences by tossing some tiny coins into my blanket. I acted as a relief for their guilt about over-charging neighbors at their shops and other ill-gotten money that was stuffed in their pockets. Oh, well, I thought, everyone has a job in society; I had found mine.

    One day as I sat begging, I heard someone call to me: Bartimaeus, why don't you find Jesus of Nazareth and ask him to cure you? It is said that Jesus has cured many people including some who are blind like you. I sensed a mocking tone in the unknown voice. The voice continued, if you were cured, Bartimaeus, you could then quit your daily begging and find a real job that provided a wage. You should ask this magician Jesus to work his magic on your eyes so we wouldn't have to see your ugly face around here anymore. Over the years, I had gotten a pretty thick skin so the taunts of those who disdained my begging didn't bother me. But these particular words were especially hateful. While I could not see, I felt the stinging in the corners of my eyes from the salty tears that had formed there. I lashed back at the voice, why don't you just move on and leave me alone. Your black soul is as dark as the insides of my eyes. I heard my blanket being disrupted followed by the clanging of the accumulated coins on the brick road where I sat. I groped around on the roadway trying to locate all the coins that had been kicked off my blanket.

Instead of being angry I was grateful to the vile person who taunted me and scattered my coins. At least he had introduced me to Jesus the prophet. From that day onward, I asked every passer by what he or she knew about Jesus. I heard a lot of interesting things. Apparently, Jesus had been traveling throughout the region for almost three years preaching a message of love of God, love of neighbor and a new way of living life. His mission had gathered many followers but the Roman and Jewish establishment feared and hated him. Many cures and miracles were attributed to Jesus and some stories were almost beyond belief. According to many reports, Jesus cured sick people, brought the dead back to life, cast out demons and fed thousands of people with a handful of food. The most amazing claim about Jesus was that he was truly the long hoped for Messiah, the Son of David who would restore Israel to its past glory and free the people from the onerous yoke of Roman occupation. My religious background was minimal but I was intrigued with Jesus. First, was he more than a mere man? Second, if I were to somehow meet him, could he possibly cure my blindness? I continued to inquire about him.

Jesus Face-To-Face

Finally, I heard that Jesus was on his way from Galilee to Jerusalem. His route would take him through Jericho. I made arrangements with a neighbor who was making a delivery in Jericho to hitch a ride on his donkey cart so I could finally hear Jesus with my own ears. We arrived in the mid-morning and, with the help of some locals, I positioned myself on the side of the road where Jesus was sure to pass. I began begging figuring that a newcomer like me might attract some more generous souls than those I met routinely in my own village. After a couple of hours sitting there—I had collected quite a few coins, thank you—I heard a commotion approaching on the road. There was general excitement; Jesus of Nazareth was coming! Others told me that he was walking, surrounded by a horde of people trying to get his attention. I could hear the garbled talk of a hundred voices, all vying to get Jesus' consideration. Begging had taught me how to use my voice effectively. I could hear the people leading the group ahead of Jesus announcing to all along the road that Jesus of Nazareth was approaching. I began my strong, high-pitched wail calling out: Jesus, Son of David, have pity on me. Over and over I repeated, Jesus, Son of David have pity on me. When the crescendo of noise was loudest, I surmised that Jesus was directly adjacent to me on the side of the road. I hoped that using the description, Son of David, might attract his notice. By calling Jesus Son of David I was acknowledging my belief that Jesus was the true Messiah. Did I believe that myself? At that moment, I wasn't convinced. Those around Jesus were yelling at me to be quiet and stop bothering him. I would not be silent. All the more I said, Jesus, Son of David have pity on me. Suddenly, I heard the crowd go quiet. I heard a man's voice saying, bring this beggar to me. I felt the strong grip of men on each side of me lifting me up to my feet and pulling me onto the road. I could not tell what was happening. The men let go of my arms. Blind people have a sense of when there are other people nearby; I strongly felt a presence. Then, after a few moments, I heard a strong but gentle voice say, I am Jesus. Why have you called me Son of David? I felt myself trembling as I formed my reply. Sir, I called you Son of David because I have been told you are the Christ, the Messiah sent down from heaven. Again a pause. Jesus then said slowly and softly, Bartimaeus, do you believe this yourself or only because others have told you so? Now it was my turn to pause. I wasn't sure how to respond to Jesus. At that moment, I felt a small explosion in my head. Everything suddenly became calm. I said, yes, Jesus, I do believe you are the Christ. I could hear others in the crowd murmuring. Then Jesus changed the subject: Bartimaeus, what do you want me to do for you? I responded, my words full of emotion, Lord, please let me see. Jesus then took his hands and gently touched my eyes. He said to me, Bartimaeus, your faith has saved you. I have given you sight.

How can I possibly describe to you what happened next? Standing there in the road, I turned my head and saw people, trees, donkeys, the sky, clouds…and a tall, handsome man grinning at me. I could see for the first time in my life! Can you imagine how I felt? The people in the crowd were jumping for joy, praising God and raising their arms to heaven in thanksgiving for the miracle they had just witnessed. Did you hear me? I could see! I began to dance and praise God like the others while Jesus looked on in amusement at the scene around him. I took the coins in my blanket and dropped them into the hand of another beggar along the road. Then I lead the parade of people towards Jericho praising God and telling everyone who would listen what had just happened to me. I was blind, but now I can see! Jesus the Christ has just cured me! Glory be to God in heaven and to the Messiah he has sent among us, I shouted. I spent the next several days with Jesus repeating my story to all within hearing distance. This next week was the happiest few days of my life.

Little did I know when Jesus cured me, he was entering the final week of his earthly life. You have all heard the account of those last days in Jerusalem; I shall not repeat the details here. Our sadness at his death was soon replaced with awe and wonder as we heard of his resurrection from the dead and many appearances in the region. I have come to believe deeply that Jesus was truly the Son of God, the Christ, the Messiah sent into the world. I will spend the rest of my life telling that story to everyone I meet.

At the beginning, I told you my story was going to be short. It turned out to be longer than I planned, but I had to tell you *everything* about my wonderful, though brief, encounter with my friend, Jesus of Nazareth, the Son of David, the Christ. I saw him with my own eyes.

The expression, to see things clearly, has a couple of meanings. To those possessing 20/20 vision, the phrase denotes the ability to perceive visually things with perfect clarity without the aid of eyeglasses. The saying also means one can identify all the aspects and nuances of a human situation and process them without distorting the truth. Because of Jesus' intervention, Bartimaeus was blessed with a miracle that permitted him to physically see things clearly. It is the other meaning of the phrase that gives some of us difficulty. When trying to understand the relationship with another human being, we can make misjudgments because we don't take time to discern the real feelings of the other person. Have you ever had someone become angry with you during a conversation and you didn't have a clue why? Could it be that your words might have been hurtful to the other person, something you did not clearly see? Have you ever failed to see how someone might be affected by your words or actions? If that has caused pain or hurt feelings it is often the result of not seeing things clearly.

While Bartimaeus asked Jesus for his physical sight, it might be wise for us to ask Jesus to see things clearly as it relates to our dealings with others. Let us all ask God to give us gentle and kind words to speak to our neighbors, words that are full of love and care and consideration for the feelings of other people. Thoughtlessness, often caused by the inability to see things clearly, creates a lot of unhappiness in our world. By asking for this blessing, we may contribute to a kinder, gentler and happier world. Lord, please let me see...clearly.

MALCHUS, THE HIGH PRIEST'S SERVANT
Matthew 26: 51
Mark 14: 47
Luke 22: 51
John 18: 10 – 11

There is little about my early life that you would find interesting. Suffice to say, my father and grandfather before him both made careers serving the political and religious leaders of the Jewish people as advisors and confidantes. As a matter of fact my given name actually means "counselor." It seems my father was grooming me from birth to follow him into service of our nation's leaders.

That is exactly the way things turned out. My first job was being an errand boy for a chief rabbi in Judea. I was diligent, aggressive and reliable so I moved up quickly. By my mid-twenties I was on the staff of the high priest in Jerusalem. Granted, I had very minor duties but I always did the best in the job I currently had. I believed that doing any task well, however minor, was a smart thing to do. This strategy seemed to work; I continued to advance in both responsibility and influence. When I was thirty, the high priest, Caiaphas, promoted me to his inner circle of advisors. I was told that my new job was to serve as the information gatherer. My portfolio included traveling around Israel, carefully listening to local leaders, finding out what issues were important to them, being alert to the rise of potential rivals to the high priest and identifying people who seemed to have a growing influence in the community. In simple words, I was "the ear" of the high priest. I took this assignment very seriously and was careful to report in great detail but never embellishing the facts as they were. As a wise and shrewd man, Caiaphas had other people doing the same job I had. He quickly learned that I was a thorough and accurate reporter and seemed to invest more trust in me as time went on.

My growing influence with Caiaphas was noticed by many in the temple precincts. In the city and surrounding areas, I was treated with great respect and was often invited to special meetings and banquets. I enjoyed the attention but was wary about letting down my guard with people who were currying favor with the high priest's confidante. It was obvious that many people were seeking my attention in hope of getting to the high priest through me. I was too clever to let that happen.

One week I traveled to Galilee to gather information about the northern region of Israel. While there, I heard about an emerging young preacher named Jesus of Nazareth. I was told he had begun his public ministry about two years ago. He had grown up in Nazareth, the son of a carpenter, but had moved to Capernaum recently with his mother. Apparently he had attracted a number of followers. Jesus had been credited by reliable sources to have performed many cures, expelled demons and achieved some incredible miracles. This was very significant news; I gathered as many facts as possible and quickly returned to Jerusalem to brief Caiaphas.

The high priest was interested in my report and listened carefully as I unfolded the situation. He did not seem particularly concerned since many young prophets had come and gone in Galilee over the past several years. However, he directed me to keep my ear to the ground and give him updates about Jesus as new information became available.

I had a broad circle of acquaintances and sources who fed me information. The more I heard about Jesus, the more I considered him a potential problem. This man was not subtle. He was calling the scribes, Pharisees and Sadducees awful names like hypocrites, white washed tombs and vipers. He was routinely pointing out how these Jewish leaders preached one thing but did something completely opposite. The common folks seemed to love Jesus but not the leaders; they were furious with him. In addition to this, Jesus and his followers seemed to flaunt the Mosaic and Talmudic law that Jews had held sacred for centuries. This new cult routinely violated the Sabbath, and did not strictly follow dietary laws. Worst of all, Jesus associated with prostitutes, tax collectors and other low-lifes and held them up as God's most loved people. No wonder the Jewish elite class was annoyed. Even the Roman authorities were beginning to understand that Jesus posed a threat to civil order. While he did not seem to be preaching the overthrow of the occupiers, he always put the needs of the poor and oppressed people first. I heard that the Romans wanted the Jewish authorities to deal with Jesus before they had to, but he consistently defeated them in the war of ideas, often making them appear foolish in their positions.

Caiaphas became restive and very uneasy with each new report I gave him. A harmless little Galilean preacher was one thing, but Jesus was making big inroads against the establishment—of which Caiaphas was a principal member. The high priest ordered me to begin shadowing Jesus so I could hear his preaching and see for myself what effect he was having. Unspoken but implicit in the order was a demand that I make a solid case against Jesus so he could be dealt with once and for all. For the first time, I felt uneasiness and trepidation about my own position. I sensed Caiaphas had ordered me to gather evidence to convict Jesus of blasphemy, heresy or worse—and don't come back here until the job is completed.

I found Jesus preaching near the Sea of Galilee. I stayed on the fringe of the crowd and avoided bringing attention to myself. In spite of this, Jesus made eye contact with me several times. Did he know who I was and the purpose of my mission? I could not help being drawn to him. He was very charismatic, a wonderful speaker and quite persuasive. He also frightened me because he posed a threat to my patron, Caiaphas. I followed him day after day. He was making outrageous statements like I am the bread of life; I am the way, the truth and the life; come to me all you who are heavily burdened and I will give you rest. Who did he think he was? God? I wasn't fooled by his preaching through parables. He was claiming to be the Son of God, the Messiah, the Holy One, the Son of David. No mere man can make those statements and get away with it. I scribbled furiously into my journal. This Jesus was a very dangerous man. He had to be stopped. But, how?

I began to observe carefully those who were closest to Jesus. There was one who seemed to demonstrate unusual body language. He appeared to disagree often with the message Jesus was giving to his followers. I found out his name was Judas Iscariot. At the end of the day, I spoke to Judas in a friendly, non-threatening way. I told him how impressed I was with those who had stepped forward to support this new prophet. I commented that he seemed especially influential and must be a very close friend of Jesus. Judas was wary at first but soon warmed up to me. He was obviously pleased with my compliments and seemed to enjoy our conversation. I worked hard to reinforce his own sense of importance and continued to treat him with great respect and deference. He was very nicely falling into the trap I was setting for him.

Following Jesus was easy. He was always surrounded by large crowds of mostly enthusiastic supporters. Often the local political and religious leaders would come out, mainly to challenge the ideas Jesus was espousing. At every stop along the way, I witnessed Jesus skewering these skeptics, but he never did in a vicious or mean-spirited way. He merely told them their ideas were wrong or that they were saying one thing but doing something entirely different. No wonder they resented Jesus so deeply. After about one week, I had accumulated enough statements to charge Jesus with blasphemy from a religious perspective and treason from a political one. I was sure Caiaphas could take decisive action based on my findings. I still needed a way to isolate Jesus from his devoted followers so we could take him into custody. I was confident I could enlist Judas to help me with this final detail.

Jesus and his entourage were heading to Jerusalem to celebrate Passover. Along the way, the crowds became larger and more excited about his preaching and cures. I continued to engage Judas whenever I could, offering blandishments about how powerful and influential I thought he was. Just before Jesus entered the Holy City, I told Judas it was important for the high priest to speak with Jesus privately. Since we did not know Jesus' whereabouts I asked Judas if he could let me know so I could inform Caiaphas and arrange a meeting between the two of them. Judas supported that idea. He believed Jesus must convince Caiaphas about certain issues. Judas also felt Jesus needed to go easier on the Jewish elite if he was ever to assume a role of power in the country. I set up a meeting between Judas and Caiaphas that was also attended by several of the high priest's functionaries. It was agreed that Judas would lead us to Jesus after the Passover meal on Thursday night. He was given a fee of thirty silver coins for his service. Caiaphas congratulated Judas for his good work and important contribution in arranging this meeting between Jesus and the high priest. The trap had been perfectly set. Jesus was as good as done.

Completing his part of the deal, Judas showed up at the palace about one hour after sunset on the appointed night. He led a group of us to a garden outside the city gates where he said Jesus was praying after celebrating Passover with his disciples. I told Judas that the presence of a squad of armed soldiers was necessary to keep the peace in case any followers of Jesus got unruly. He appeared uneasy about this but said nothing as we set out.

It was a very dark night. The torches carried by several of our party cast eerie shadows as we approached the appointed place. Suddenly, the dim light illuminated Jesus. Judas approached him and gave Jesus a fleeting kiss saying, hail, Rabbi. Jesus seemed to look past Judas and addressed the rest of us: whom do you seek? As the high priest's chief servant, I responded, Jesus the Nazorean. Jesus said, I AM he. With those words all in our party tumbled to the ground as if hit by a devastating blast of wind. Perhaps it was the words I AM. To Jews, this is a designation for God. But I'm speculating. I will never really know why we all fell down at the same time. It is a mystery. We recovered quickly and scrambled to our feet. Again I took the lead and said, Jesus, you are under arrest. You will be taken to the palace of the high priest to undergo questioning. Several of Jesus' followers appeared out of the darkness thinking they might protect and defend him. One particularly burly fellow brandished a knife he had pulled out of his belt. This knife wielder yelled, leave Jesus alone! He seemed crazed with anger toward us and made several slashing thrusts with his dagger. I was standing too close to him, and suddenly I felt intense pain on the right side of my head. I raised my hand to the point of my distress to feel that my right ear had been severed from my head and blood was gushing from the wound. As I crumpled to the ground, I heard Jesus say to his friend, put your sword back into its sheath. All who take up the sword shall also perish by the sword. Don't you think I could call upon my father and he would provide me with more than twelve legions of angels to protect me? Let the scriptures be fulfilled.

As I lay in agony on the ground, Jesus knelt down beside me and gently reached out his left hand to touch my head. Jesus said to me, I remember seeing you in Galilee. I'm sorry that you have been injured tonight. He was smiling kindly at me and his fingers were soothing. Suddenly, the pain I had been feeling disappeared. I reached up with my hand to my ear. It had been completely restored! My severed ear that had been on the ground was now reattached to my head. There was no more blood. The pain was gone. Jesus had apparently cured me, one of his most bitter antagonists.

As the soldiers and others took Jesus away to the palace, I remained alone in the garden. My blood soaked tunic was the only reminder of the horrible injury I had suffered. I felt terribly conflicted about this event. A man I hated had taken time to heal my wound. Was he just a man? Was the information I had gathered about him true after all? Was he the Messiah, the Son of David? Was Jesus actually I AM?

After witnessing the events of Friday including Jesus from the cross proclaiming, Father forgive them for they know not what they do, I sat down and wrote Caiaphas a letter of resignation. My enthusiasm for the job had disappeared. While I did not feel converted to a Jesus follower, I had heard him say many things that resonated with me. Jesus said, blessed are the merciful for they will be shown mercy. Caiaphas never said that. Jesus said, whoever loses his life for my sake will find it. Caiaphas never said that. Jesus said, whatever you do for these least brothers and sisters, you did for me. Caiaphas never said that. Jesus said, what profit is there for one to gain the whole world and forfeit his life. Caiaphas never said that either. I had a lot of time ahead of me to sort out all my feelings. How ironic that I was "the ear" for Caiaphas and Jesus healed my ear in the garden on that dark Thursday evening. I will never be the same person again.

Greg Hadley

How many times has each of us been healed physically? An accident, a fall, a cut received from broken glass, a serious medical procedure—none of us has completely escaped some bodily wounds. Good doctors providing proper medical attention may start us back on the road to recovery. Our amazing bodies perform their miraculous healing cycles and, before you know it, cuts, scrapes and gashes are restored to "as new" condition. But what about our emotional, psychological and spiritual wounds? They are often more difficult to heal. Angry outbursts among family members, total rejection by a loved and trusted friend, a dark secret revealed by someone seeking revenge—these and similar things can leave our spirits bruised, battered and horribly wounded. If not tended to and eventually mended, these injuries never seem to heal leaving us with a festering, jagged scar on our soul. Malchus needed divine help to be cured and so do we. What words can possibly be harder to say? I am sorry; please forgive me; overlook my thoughtlessness; I want to be reconciled to you—what can I do to make that happen? When said, those words often burn our throats and scald our tongues. Yes, we also require God's help to forgive others when they have hurt us. In this respect we must join Malchus at the foot of the cross where he heard Jesus say, Father, forgive them for they know not what they do. It may be hard to say these words but we do well to emulate Jesus. Forgive us our trespasses as we forgive others who trespass against us. This is our daily prayer.

JOHN, THE BOY WITH THE LOAVES AND FISH
Matthew 14: 12 – 21
Mark 6: 31 – 44
Luke 9: 10 – 17
John 6: 5 – 15

As a boy of thirteen, my parents permit me to be away from home without their direct supervision. That is better than when I was just a couple of years younger. Then I had to be within earshot of their calls. Now they trust me to be out and about and I like it much better. That means I can explore the nearby areas with my friends. I never go too far or abuse my freedom, but it does make me feel somewhat independent and grown up.

One of the things my friends and I have been doing is tagging along with the crowds of people going to hear the prophet Jesus of Nazareth. Some of these gatherings attract huge numbers of people. I've never seen so many human beings at one time in my young life. The handful of men Jesus counts as his main disciples are very busy during these large assemblies. They are trying to protect Jesus from being mobbed, directing people so there are no conflicts or crushes and trying to insure there is water available for all attending. My little group of teenage boys eagerly volunteers to help out the disciples with little chores like fetching water. They seem to be very grateful for the assistance. Once in awhile they will even slip us a small coin from the treasury bag for the work we do. It is fun for us, keeps us occupied and out of trouble, plus we sometimes get paid. We think that is a pretty happy situation for us. I have been doing this for about six months now. While I have not met Jesus personally, I have heard him speak. He seems so nice and he's smart too. All of my friends have decided that we would enjoy being like Jesus when we are grown up.

Most of these big gatherings with Jesus turn out to be all day affairs. Of course, I always tell my mother in advance when I plan to attend one of the meetings Jesus has with the people. When she knows I am going to be gone all day, she prepares a lunch for me. Usually the food consists of small biscuits made of barley flour. Because we are pretty poor, we only have barley in our house. Those who have more money all eat bread or biscuits made of wheat flour, but our income doesn't allow us the luxury of buying wheat flour. Most of the rich people in our village feed barley to their animals so that gives you an idea about our economic status in the community.

I love to help my mother prepare the small barley loaves or biscuits as I call them. Mother normally makes six of these little loaves at a time. Her recipe calls for about two measures of barley flour, a little salt, three-quarters of a cup of water and a couple of spoons full of olive oil. If they are available in our cupboard, mother will include a small handful of seeds like sunflowers and a little honey if my father has found a comb while he is out working. All these ingredients are kneaded together and rolled out about one-half inch thick. Mother then lets me use a cup upside down to form five little round biscuits. The scrap dough is gathered up, rolled again and a sixth and final biscuit is formed. The loaves are then put into a hot oven for about forty minutes. I love the smell in our house as the bread bakes. When taken out of the oven, the biscuits are a golden brown and quite crunchy on the outside. I must admit they are not nearly as tasty as bread made from wheat flour but they still satisfy my palate very well. In addition to the bread, mother sends me out with a couple of dried fish. We buy these from the local fishmonger. They are sardines about five inches long. Mother normally dries these fish on the window ledge of our kitchen. Sometimes she will use some cheap wine vinegar to pickle the fish. Either way, they are salty and have a taste pleasing to me. When I head out on one of my daylong excursions, I am well supplied with food that I carry in a little bag. Along with a skin filled with water, I can make it through the day even with my expansive teenage appetite. Mother is very considerate of my needs, and I love her for the way she takes care of me.

Just before another big gathering was planned, all in our community were shocked to hear that the Tetrarch Herod had beheaded John the Baptist. According to reports, John was a cousin of Jesus and had actually baptized Jesus in the Jordan River. John was very popular. After his death it was assumed that Jesus would take up John's mantle as a voice crying out in the desert. All the people in the area were terribly disheartened by the Baptist's death and were looking for solace and comfort from the preaching of Jesus.

Again mother prepared the bread and fish for my lunch with a little help from me. I kissed her and then headed out to the open space where I was told Jesus would speak this day. Well before noon it was apparent that this multitude of people would be the biggest ever. I'm not sure that I know how to estimate numbers of people, but my friends and I thought there must be close to fifteen thousand people gathered in a large meadow to hear Jesus. I could be wrong about the estimate but there were a huge number of men, women and children assembled this day. As always, my friends and I volunteered to help the disciples with their mundane chores. All of them appreciated us but Peter seemed especially thankful for our help. We all kept busy throughout the afternoon, so busy that we didn't really hear Jesus speak or take a break. I had gotten hungry at mid-day so I stopped working for a brief moment and reached into my bag for a biscuit, which I ate along with taking a drink of water. It took the edge off my appetite.

As late afternoon arrived signaling the end of the day, I noticed all the disciples in a huddle around Jesus.

Everyone looked quite serious. After a short time, the disciples began fanning out into the crowd talking to the people. One of Jesus' disciples, Philip, approached me and said, John, did you bring any food with you today? Yes, Philip, I responded. My mother prepared a simple lunch of barley cakes and fish for me. Why do you ask? Philip said, we are searching for food to feed this large crowd. Please come with me while I speak to Jesus. I followed Philip through the crowds and, for the first time, I found myself standing right next to Jesus. Up close he was a very impressive man. Philip introduced me to him. Rabbi, this boy is John. He often helps us with gatherings like this. He tells me that his mother sent him here today with some barley cakes and fish. Philip continued, it is all the food we can find, Master, and is totally inadequate to fill our needs. Jesus looked at me and took his hand to tousle the hair on my head. I am happy to meet you, young man, he said. Thanks for all the help you and your friends have been to my followers. Would you be willing to share your food with others today, Jesus asked? I couldn't understand how my little portion of food could possibly help with feeding this crowd. I was also starting to get really hungry so I was a little hesitant to give up my meager lunch. But, this powerful man had asked me to do so. How could I refuse him? Of course, Jesus, if you need my food, I will share it, I told him. I also told him sheepishly that I had already eaten one of the barley cakes. He looked at me and smiled. You're a great kid, Jesus said. Your parents must be proud of you and your generous spirit. My cheeks flushed when hearing those nice words and I grinned back at Jesus.

I heard him give orders to his disciples to organize the throng into manageable groups so that food could be distributed in an orderly way. The crowd was quite malleable so it didn't take long to set up the divisions of about one hundred men each. As this was happening, Jesus said to me, John, will you be willing to help my friends distribute the food to the people in the groups? Yes sir, I responded. I will be happy to help. Can my friends help, too? Of course, Jesus said. I handed my small lunch bag to Jesus. I watched as he reached in and took out one biscuit and a fish. Lifting his eyes to heaven he said, Father, bless this simple food and let it provide physical nourishment to all those who have come here today. He continued: bless those who have provided this meal to their neighbors in an act of unselfish love. At that, Jesus began handing the food to his disciples. Each time he reached into the bag, his hand withdrew another cake and fish. I was amazed at what I saw. Finally it was my turn to take some food to distribute it to the people. The bag seemed to hold an inexhaustible supply of cakes and fish. I was dumbstruck.

The disciples, my friends and I were shuttling back and forth between Jesus and the multitude of people distributing food to them and their families. While no one else had admitted to having food with them, I did observe several families who began sharing hidden caches of food and drink with their neighbors. They must have been inspired by Jesus' generosity. This episode went on for almost one hour until every single person had been fed to their satisfaction. Jesus then directed his disciples to retrieve the leftovers so that nothing would be wasted. Many wicker baskets were filled with fragments of barley biscuits and dried fish.

When this was all over, I was still near Jesus. Self-consciously I asked him, Jesus how were you able to feed all those people with the little I gave you? He responded in a subdued voice, sounding suddenly weary from the work he had just done. John, he said, one message of my preaching is about abundance. Abundance of God's love for every human being, abundance of each person's love for their neighbors and abundance of blessings for everyone as they travel life's journey to salvation. What you saw today was an example of the profusion of my love for my people. You made an important contribution to today's message. Thank you, young friend, for your willingness to help me when your generosity was sorely needed.

Can you possibly imagine the tale I told after arriving home that evening? The story about the events of the day just tumbled out of my mouth as I tried to share everything I had seen, heard and experienced. My parents listened carefully to what I said, occasionally interrupting to ask a question. While they loved and trusted me, I'm sure they felt parts of my story were exaggerated or embellished. At the end, mother gently asked me, John, do you really believe that Jesus fed fifteen thousand people with the handful of food I gave you this morning? I responded, mother, I don't have any idea how it happened but I know what I saw with my own eyes. People say that Jesus has performed miracles. Perhaps I saw one of his miracles today. My mother hugged me for a long time as we both pondered what had happened this day in Galilee.

Now, years later, I still hold Jesus in a special place in my heart. Although he is physically gone, his presence lives on through the Holy Spirit in his church. Over and over again I have experienced the generosity of his love and the abundance of graces that he promised. Praise be to Jesus the Christ!

Many of us frequently use the metaphor about the glass half empty or the glass half full to explain feelings about optimism or the adequacy of our resources. In 2 Corinthians 9: 6-10 we hear that those who sow sparingly shall also reap sparingly. On the other hand those who sow bountifully will reap bountifully. Moreover, God is able to give us every grace abundantly that we need to be his faithful followers. All too often, we worry about scarcity. We don't have enough time, adequate financial resources or hearts big enough to love everyone we should. The Holy Spirit wants us to know that there are copious blessings available to each of us to help us live our lives. Our God is a

God of abundance not scarcity. John, the young boy in our story, saw this first hand. For the rest of us we must come to believe that God never runs out of love or blessings or help for anyone of us who turns to Him in time of need. Our God is a generous God.

Greg Hadley

CAIUS, A CENTURION AND HIS SLAVE
Matthew 8: 5 – 13
Luke 7: 1 – 10

Previously in this book, my young friend Antonias has told a story about his personal grim encounter with Jesus of Nazareth. During the course of that story, Antonias spoke about me in some detail. He served under me as a young officer in the Roman army. I considered myself as his mentor. I believed he had bright prospects for a career in the military service. I am not going to recover ground that Antonias has written about. It is important for me to tell you that it was I who told Antonias about my encounter with Jesus. Until then, Antonias had never heard of him. Perhaps my comrade never would have met the great prophet if it were not for me. Who knows?

I will pick up the story after Antonias left my command and headed for a tour in Israel with his new unit. Soon thereafter, my unit also received orders to ship out to Israel but our assignment was in the north near Capernaum. That was a much more agreeable place to work and live. Prior to departure, I took a ship south across Mare Nostrum to a city on the North African coast named Tripoli. There I purchased a male slave. I had always wanted to have a permanent servant that I controlled completely. The purchase of a slave in Tripoli's slave market was the best way to make that happen.

I do not intend to debate you about the practicality, morality or ethics of owning another human being. It was legal for me to own a slave; it suited my purposes at the time and so I did it. I suppose it can be argued that the young black man I purchased lacked culture, manners or education of any sort. Based on an objective comparison to a man like myself—cultured, educated, influential and well bred—the slave seemed obviously inferior in almost every respect. Please do not be mistaken: I did not consider my slave to be sub-human. I could see that he had an intellect, although poorly developed, displayed human feelings of joy, sorrow, fear, interest, boredom and desire and possessed all the human appetites for food, drink, rest, love and interaction with other people. Yes, he was a human being just like me. Well, not exactly just like me, but very close at least on a fundamental level.

My slave surely had a name in his village. I renamed him Orsonero, which means black bear. He was truly a big, hulking man. About eighteen years old, he was at least six feet tall and with a large, muscular frame. He appeared to be very strong, but I also sensed a subdued gentleness about him from the very beginning. Being a centurion's slave was probably not his first choice for a life's career, but he seemed resigned to this fate. When the transaction for his sale was complete, he followed me compliantly. We had initial difficulty with communication but we soon learned some signs and basic words that allowed us to understand each other. The trip back to Rome was interesting. Orsonero had never been at sea before. He was invigorated by the ocean air but wary and fearful about what might await him if he stepped off the wooden deck into the churning blue-green water. His eyes were wide with wonder. Everything he was seeing and experiencing was obviously new to him.

In Rome, I began to train Orsonero on the most basic level. He needed to be taught to wash his hands, bathe daily, to toilet hygienically and change and launder his clothing. He absorbed things very quickly; I was pleased with his rapid progress on all the fundamental chores. Each day I expanded his list of things to complete. He remained eager to learn and seemed to actually enjoy much of the work he was given to do. By nature, I remain aloof from my subordinates and I made it clear to Orso from the beginning that he and I were never going to become friends in the classic sense. Still, we seemed to develop an easy relationship. He consistently deferred to my position of authority while I treated him with demanding strictness, but also basic human respect. Slave or not, I had to begrudgingly admit, I liked Orso (I frequently shortened his name to simply "Bear").

Orso was a great help to me in the move of my unit to Israel. Each day our ability to communicate with each other improved. His language skills were excellent and soon he had a good grasp of Romanized Latin, the common vernacular of the Roman army. While I seldom permitted Orso to eat with me, occasionally I would let him sit on the floor of my dining pavilion while I had my evening meal. He knew never to speak unless first spoken to by me. I liked to ask him questions about his family and village. He was animated when talking about the life he left behind. He was especially fond of his mother, wistfully telling me stories about how she cared for and loved him. One day when speaking of her again, Orso's eyes filled with tears. He, no doubt, missed her very much. While he never mentioned it, I'm sure he knew he would never see his mother again.

My duties in Capernaum took on an easy pace sometimes edging on boredom. I believed one of my jobs was to maintain good relationships with the local people. I frequently met with the town political leaders and also with the temple officials. Although I had no religious interest of any sort, I knew the temple was a center for community activity and most important to many in the area. Orso was now competent and trained to perform a host of chores around my quarters and my soldiers' camp. I liked his even disposition and the fact he seldom caused trouble. Once in awhile he would exhibit temper, frustration with a task or sulk. Then I would be forced to discipline him. Never did I beat him. I would restrict him from food he especially liked or limit his freedom to move about, but never did I strike him. In that respect he was treated better than some of the soldiers under my command. Orso and I had settled into our respective roles quite nicely with only one big difference: I was free and he was not. That was an enormous gulf, I thought.

One day, I noticed Orsonero was quite listless. He seemed unfocused and lacking energy. I looked him in the eye; in return I received a dull stare. I placed my hand on his forehead and immediately knew that Orso had a high fever. Obviously, he was ill. I ordered my orderlies to put him to bed and minister to him as if he were one of my soldiers. The response from these men was markedly unenthusiastic. Their silence and body language spoke volumes: you expect us to take care of this big black slave of yours and nurse him back to health? I knew what was on their minds; I sternly ordered them to fulfill my command and let them know they would be held harshly accountable if I found any slacking in performance.

Soon after Orso took sick, I discovered two important facts: I really missed Orso's service and his companionship, too. Though loathe to admit it, he had become much more than a slave to me. This realization made me feel uneasy; I was having trouble processing my own emotions about the man. While completing my duties one day, I encountered the local rabbi. I mentioned Orso's illness. The rabbi offhandedly mentioned that a local young prophet named Jesus was known to perform many cures. He asked me if I would like more details about the prophet or if there was any help the temple or its members could provide. I had an especially good relationship with the temple and had actually given them some assistance with a building project they were doing. While grateful for his suggestion, I would never seriously consider using some kind of shaman or witch doctor to treat my friend, er, my slave.

Except, Orso wasn't getting any better. In fact, he appeared to be getting sicker each day. Why should I worry, I asked myself? He's a slave; if something happens, I will just buy another slave. I was deluding myself. Orsonero had become important to me as a person and I was worried that his illness was leading to death. I revisited the local rabbi. Could you send someone from the temple to talk to Jesus to see if he might be willing to visit my slave, I asked? Of course, the rabbi answered, seeing my deep concern for Orsonero. Thank you, rabbi, I replied. Please ask this Jesus to come quickly. The situation demanded that I shed my pretense about shamans. Maybe this Jesus could actually help. I had to find out.

The next evening, the rabbi came to my quarters. He told me that several senior members of the temple had found Jesus and informed him about the situation with my slave. Jesus had promised to come this way tomorrow morning. I was very grateful for this assistance. Early the next morning I was on the road that led into Capernaum. As a matter of courtesy, I wanted to go out and meet Jesus to introduce myself and thank him for coming to assist Orsonero. About nine o'clock, I saw a small entourage of people heading toward me. Leading the group was a tall, handsome figure. Some people in my party identified this person as Jesus of Nazareth. I dismounted my horse and approached Jesus, my hand extended to greet him. Jesus, I said, I am Caius. I am most grateful that you have come to help. My slave Orsonero is gravely ill I fear, and I don't know where to turn. Let me be honest, Jesus, I am not a man who holds religious beliefs so I have no understanding or expectation that you as a mere man can offer medical relief. Jesus listened to me and then said to me, smiling, Caius, I have heard from my Jewish brothers in Capernaum that you have been a thoughtful and considerate friend to their community. We don't often receive that kind of treatment from Roman soldiers and I want you to know how much we appreciate your kindness. I want to help your friend Orsonero and will be pleased to come to your quarters to see him. I found this man Jesus to be very compelling. He was bright, articulate and exuded a gentle kindness. Listening to Jesus inspired me to make the following statement to him: Master, I am not worthy to have you enter under my roof. I believe that you only need to say the word and Orsonero will be healed. I then continued, like you I am a person of authority with many soldiers reporting to me. I say to one go and he goes; to another come here and he comes; and to my slave do this and he does it. I'm sure you can understand what I am saying, Jesus. I have no idea how I formed these words and had no intention of saying things like this to Jesus. From what part of my brain this statement came, I will never know. He listened carefully to my comments then turned and said to his entourage, never before in Israel have I found such faith. Jesus then turned and looked at me intently for several moments. He finally said to me in a soft voice, Caius, you can now go home. Because of your belief, I have answered your request. Your slave Orsonero is healed. Jesus then reached out and embraced me. I was not used to this show of affection, but Jesus hugged me warmly. I could not help but hug him back. Finally, he stepped away, smiled at me again and said, Caius I am pleased that we have met. I wish you good luck. Please continue to take good care of the Jewish community in Capernaum. I hope to see you again some time. With that, he turned and began heading down the road away from the town.

    I immediately ordered two of my soldiers to return to my quarters at a fast gallop. They were to determine the health status of Orso and come back to let me know. Within an hour the messengers were back informing me that Orsonero had suddenly and completely recovered from his malady and appeared to be feeling fine. I rode the rest of the way back to my quarters in silence, trying to process what had just taken place.

Arriving at the infirmary, I immediately visited Orso. He looked tired but seemed his old self in every other respect. I am well, Master. What has happened to me, he said? I don't really know, Orso, I told him, but I believe you have received your cure from a very special person, a man named Jesus. I am very grateful to that man and even more so now that you are restored to health. I order you to rest, I said in a mock serious voice. Goodnight, Master Caius, Orso said. Thank you for helping me get well.

Upon returning to my office, I wrote a letter to young Antonius, which he details in his story. My intellect still was not clearly processing the events of today. Was Orso cured by some unseen hand of a higher power? What role did Jesus play in the totally unexpected recovery of my slave? If Jesus had some magical curative powers, why did he exercise them on my behalf, a non-religious, non-believing man? What faith did I exhibit that he found so remarkable? I could not connect my thoughts in a logical way that made sense to me. That night, I lay upon my cot reflecting upon Jesus' embrace as I finally drifted off to sleep.

I was due some home leave in Rome. Orso and I boarded a ship and several days later landed at Anzio a port close to Rome. Over the past several weeks I developed a plan that was a response to my newfound care and fondness for Orso. When we landed in Anzio, I gave Orso three things: a document with my seal that declared Orso to be a free man forevermore; passage on a boat headed back to Tripoli; a sack of money so he would have plenty of funds for his journey. He was stunned as I explained all of this. I said to him, Orso, you are now a free man. Never again will you be a slave. I want you to go back to your home village, find your mother and give her a big kiss for me. I hate to lose your friendship and your service but I know this is the right thing for me to do. Looking at the ground and trembling, Orso was silent for several moments. Finally, he looked up and said to me, I love you, Master Caius. You have been good to me. I will never forget you. Roman Centurions do not cry but tears welled in my eyes. I love you too, Orso. May God always protect and keep you for the rest of your life. Now go, before you miss your boat. Goodbye, Orsonero. You are part of my life, I whispered as he turned and walked down the dock toward his boat.

Caius teaches us several lessons. He exhibits understanding, compassion, honor, and willingness to change. All of these things we would do well to emulate. But, most of all, Caius shows us the power of love. He discovered that another human being has the ability to make us better in spite of ourselves. He first viewed Orsonero as merely a slave, a chattel to be used solely for the benefit of the owner. Soon, Caius felt his heart being touched as he came to know Orso as a person with loving qualities. Sometimes we find ourselves using others for our own purposes. It is then that we should be reminded of the words of Jesus: I came to serve, not to be served. In all relationships with our fellow human beings, we are well advised to adopt the following mindset: what can I do to help the other person? How can I make his or her life better? How can I demonstrate a true sense of love toward him or her?

CALEB, AND HIS POSSESED SON, GAD
Matthew 17: 14 – 20
Mark 9: 14 – 29
Luke 9: 37 – 43

I can't take it any longer. The situation seems hopeless. What have I possibly done to deserve this dreadful situation with my son, Gad? The boy has been possessed by some kind of evil spirit, of that there is no doubt. How it happened is a total mystery to me. I'm not even sure when it occurred. This has been going on since Gad was approximately seven years old. Now he is fifteen. My wife and my relationship with her have been torn apart by the demonic ranting of our boy. I have always thought of myself as a spiritual, God-fearing man who relied on prayer and frequent attendance at temple to maintain a close relationship with God. Now I feel that God has abandoned me, sitting there on his celestial throne laughing and cruelly mocking me in my misery. I am bitter, helpless and angry at God. How could he have done this to me?

The manifestation of the possession is brutally humiliating to me and my family. Suddenly, without any prior warning, Gad will throw himself to the ground, his arms and legs flailing wildly as he foams at the mouth and his eyes practically bulge out of their sockets. I have actually seen him throw himself into a fire pit or jump into deep water even though he cannot swim. At other times he would become as rigid as a piece of wood and gnash his teeth with a horrible grating sound. When this occurs, he often shrieks in a deep guttural grunting, the most vile and obscene things I have ever heard. My wife and I are mortified when this happens in public, as it frequently does. His siblings pretend that they do not know who he is. I am also convinced that our self-righteous neighbors wag their tongues and gossip behind our backs about what terrible sins I surely have committed in life to have this awful curse fall upon me.

There seems to be no hope for a cure or possibility of exorcising the demon. We have sought help from every rabbi in the entire region without success. Doctors observe Gad and merely shrug their shoulders acknowledging their futility. At this point I am actually quite frightened. The thought of doing away with Gad has become a serious fantasy for me. I feel guilt and revulsion that I let these ideas even cross my mind. It is a sign of how truly desperate I have become. I am in the depths of hell.

Our frantic search for a solution has led us to an itinerant preacher named Jesus of Nazareth and his disciples. Caravans of merchants passing through our village have brought us stories about the many cures and exorcisms this Jesus has performed. I dismissed the first few reports. Nothing travels faster than sensational gossip or exaggerated stories. When each new group of travelers seemed to report similar facts my curiosity intensified. I didn't want to get my hopes up, but in my situation I would investigate any possibility.

Jesus seemed to arrive on the scene just before the popular John the Baptist was beheaded by Herod. Many people had listened to and heeded John's call for repentance and most were terribly distraught when he was killed. Jesus seemed to emerge thereafter and quickly gathered followers. One current story being told is that John actually identified Jesus as the long sought Messiah. That sounded outlandish to me, but you know how these tales can be embellished as they pass from person to person. I was more interested in hearing about the cures and exorcisms that Jesus had performed. In my state of mind and spirit, I did not care about finding the Messiah. I just needed to have my son's curse removed. Was Jesus the Messiah? I really didn't care. I was interested in him only to the extent he could relieve me of this millstone around my neck and the neck of my son.

I decided to take Gad and go find Jesus. I had to travel with a rope tethering us together. It looked like I was leading a donkey down the road. It was necessary to proceed this way because I never knew when he would explode in one his violent outbursts. I hated the attention that this drew to me. After a couple of days of most unpleasant travel, we came across a large group of people having some kind of heated discussion on the side of the road. I inquired what was going on and was told that a number of disciples of Jesus were arguing with some local scribes and temple leaders about when the Messiah was coming and how the people would know it was he. I asked if Jesus were present. No, I was told, he was off with three of his disciples, Peter, James and John. Some bystander said that Jesus and the three men had gone to meet with Moses and Elijah. What a preposterous story! Have you ever heard such rubbish? The outrageous things I must put up with just because I am seeking relief from my son's demon!

I had come this far so I elbowed and pushed my way to the center of the group. There I found several men who others pointed out to me as principal disciples of Jesus. Sir, I said to one of them (I was later told his name was Judas Iscariot), has Jesus conferred on you the power to cast out demons? Judas and some of his companions gathered around saying to me, why do you ask this? I then passionately told the story of the evil spirit that possessed my son, Gad. I pleaded with them to help me if they could since I had reached the end of my endurance and patience. At this point, several of the disciples gathered near Gad just as he startled all in the crowd by launching into another fit. Forming a circle around Gad, the disciples held hands and began to pray, looking up to heaven as they called down blessings to expel the demon they faced. Lying on the ground, Gad was like a wild animal, trying to grab and bite the disciples' ankles and legs. After several minutes of fervent incantations, the disciples bent over and put their hands on Gad, demanding that the evil spirit leave the boy. For quite some time, Gad lay silent and motionless as the crowd hushed in expectation. Suddenly, Gad began a maniacal laugh and screamed at the disciples, you cannot defeat me! I am here to stay inside this disgusting, pitiful boy. Now, tell your God to go straight to hell himself where he will meet all my relatives. This was followed by a cascade of wild and satanic laughing.

Another utter failure I thought. Why was I so foolish to think that some backcountry preacher or his followers could possibly relieve me of my trouble? As usual, this was a total waste of my time, another blind alley, a dead end road. Will this misery never end, I wondered? Just then, there was a commotion in the crowd. I heard one of the disciples cry out, look! Here comes Jesus, Peter, and the two brothers, James and John.

I thought, this is my last chance. As Jesus approached the crowd, I cried out, Lord, have pity on my lunatic son who suffers severely. I brought him to your disciples, but they could not cure him. Jesus stood there surveying the scene before him. Gad was curled up in a fetal position at my feet. His disciples appeared embarrassed and hapless. Shaking his head in disappointment, I heard Jesus mutter to no one in particular, what a faithless generation; how long will I be with you and endure your lack of faith? Than Jesus said, bring the poor boy to me. At that, Gad became frantic—or was it the demon who was distressed? I said to Jesus, please have compassion on us; help my son if you can. Jesus stared at me for a long time. He said to me, you ask if I can help. The real question is, are you willing to do what it takes to cure your son? I was stunned by this comment and didn't know how to respond. Jesus then continued, for the man who has faith nothing is impossible. At that moment, my eyes were opened and I saw how wrong I had been about Gad's problem. Jesus had shown me that I was worried about how Gad's demon was affecting me, not him. The whole time this poor young boy had suffered I believed it was I doing the suffering not him. I had been a selfish, self-centered egotist only concerned for my own feelings, not the agony being endured by my dear son. This revelation caused me to cry out to Jesus, I do believe, Lord; help me with my unbelief. Jesus smiled at me and nodded his head in affirmation. With that he said, evil spirit, come out of the boy and never enter him again. Gad convulsed violently then lay completely still looking as if he had died. Jesus reached down, took his hand and raised him up. Gad stood next to me calmly, grinning at all around him as he shook hands first with Jesus and then all in the crowd. In those proceeding moments, Jesus had freed Gad of the demon and returned him to a normal boy. Jesus had also shown me who I was, and I didn't like what I saw. Instead of being a loving, caring father with concern for my son, I had become worried only about my own feelings. I am not sure who received the greater cure today, Gad or me. Today's brief meeting with Jesus changed both of our lives in a wonderful and positive way. Thank you, Jesus.

Does Caleb's personal epiphany resonate with you in any way? Many of us are blind to our own selfishness. We think we are concerned with the difficulties faced by our own family, friends and loved ones. In reality, we are often more concerned with how their actions put us in a bad light or a fragile position. It can often be difficult to understand our own motives. We don't like to think that we may be selfish and self-centered. We can easily convince ourselves that our feeble attempts to help others may just be a smoke screen for our efforts to protect ourselves from any embarrassment. Developing a true sense of empathy for others is a real virtuous act. Instead of worrying about how things will affect us, we need to do our best to see how others are affected. When we become our brother's keepers and view each person as a member of the Body of Christ, we have walked a long way down the road to our personal salvation.

Greg Hadley

MOSHA, THE WOMAN CAUGHT IN ADULTERY
John 7: 53 through John 8: 11

I am full of shame for the life I have lived. Selling my body to men to satisfy their sexual gratification is the way I have earned my living for the last ten years. Was this all my fault? I can tell you about a number of factors outside my control that affected my choices. When I am completely honest with myself, however, I know I must accept full responsibility for the direction my life has taken. I hate the way I always feel dirty and degraded. The totally anonymous and faceless men I service are mostly disgusting animals who make me physically sick and give me not a scintilla of pleasure. So, why do I do it, you ask? Because *it is the only thing I know how to do*! It puts bread on my table and roof over my head. In the true sense of the word, I am good for nothing—except for providing sexual services to repulsive men.

Yes, I do have some excuses to offer for my behavior. My father treated me like dirt and never respected me while I was growing up. My mother was so spineless that she never stood up for me and remained a silent witness when I was beaten and abused by my father. My older brother and his lecherous friends used me as a plaything when I was a young girl and forced to me to do unspeakable acts for their selfish and perverse pleasure. All these things required me to grow up much too fast and left me with a hard edge to my personality. But, these are merely excuses that salve my conscience so I don't go insane with guilt. No matter how I try to parse this situation, I can only conclude that I possess a black and flinty soul that surely deserves an eternity in hell when my earthly life ends.

In spite of the repulsiveness I feel for my current life, I am also terrified about the future. What will happen to me when I am not so young and desirable as I am now? When I turn into a wrinkled, toothless hag, who will want me then? Not only is today an abomination, but tomorrow promises even more hopelessness and black despair. Woe is me! I wish I were never born.

While most people live their lives in daylight on the main roads dealing with other productive citizens, I live mine in the nighttime shadows and the narrow back alleys of the community. My clients always seem to know how to find me when I am needed. Each new encounter is filled with the prospect of terrifying danger. Countless times I have been beaten, kicked and otherwise physically abused by those who buy my services. When a client approaches me, I often wonder—will this be the one who goes into a rage and beats me to death? In my business, one must pretend to be charming and alluring in every situation. Can you imagine how hard this is for me? I seem to lurch from one crisis to another with indignity piled upon indignity. What is the absolute worst part? I cannot see a way out of this disaster called my life. Night after night, week after week, month after month I exist in this putrid, festering cesspool without ever experiencing hope that things might improve.

If nothing else, I have learned to be street wise, so what happened last night even shocked and terrified me. I was walking along an alley about twilight. A well-dressed man slowly proceeded toward me. My instincts told me there was something strange about this fellow. I was immediately wary. I continued walking, but he put out his hand to stop me. He was neither coarse nor physically aggressive. He said to me in a calm voice, I would like to speak with you for a moment. I stopped and he began to tell me a detailed story about his home life and his relationship with his wife. You can imagine that I have heard exactly the same story countless times. Naturally, the man I am talking to is always the apparent victim in these tales of marital unhappiness. If only his wife were more loving, patient, open, attentive…talk, talk, talk…everything would be just fine. In the meantime, he has all these pent up desires, and I am the only person in the world that can help him this night. The more this man spoke the less concerned I became. He appeared to be just like all the rest—hapless, clumsy, and self-centered with interest in no one except himself. In other words, he was my classic client. It took just a few moments of tawdry negotiations to agree on my fee. Then we headed for a ramshackle inn nearby where I kept a room permanently booked. I entered the room with two thoughts in mind: don't let him hurt me; make the encounter end as soon as possible. From that moment on, I only remember that everything was just the same as with the last client; nothing ever changes. I had learned long ago that sex without love is mechanical, boring, awkward and unfulfilling lust. Tonight promised to be identical to all the others I had spent in this room—until early morning when everything suddenly changed.

About ten men burst into the room and restrained me. The man I had been with all night quickly gathered up his clothes and scurried away like a rat never to be seen by me again. Meanwhile, the others were shouting vile names at me, and accusing me of committing sins against God and nature. There were both older and younger men in the group, and it was obvious they had little concern for how they handled me or my body. On the pretense of restraining me, many hands grabbed and groped me in totally inappropriate ways. While feigning their outrage at my sinfulness, they were making sure they had a little personal pleasure at my expense. I could not understand why this group had picked me to assault. What had I done to any of them, I wondered? As I heard their conversations, it became obvious that I was being used as an example to entrap some preacher with whom these men had a dispute. Observing their dress and the way they spoke, I concluded that they were learned and sophisticated men, perhaps even political or religious leaders in the community. I became terrified thinking how this morning might end. I was hearing frequent statements about the need to stone the adulteress to death, and how I was most deserving of the ultimate punishment for my sins. I heard nothing about possible punishment for the man who bought my services. He had disappeared.

The group dragged me through the streets toward the temple square in the center of town. I was given no opportunity to dress properly before we headed out, so I was half naked, completely disheveled and trembling in fear. Outside the temple, the group restraining me found the one they sought, Jesus of Nazareth. I had never heard of him but as the conversation developed, he was apparently a popular new Jewish prophet who had acquired a large following for his radical teaching about love, justice and following God's commands for our life.

This handsome young man had a sizable group of people around him. He was giving them instructions of some sort when the men pulling me arrived in the square. One of the older men in the group pushed me out into the middle. I was mortified to be seen by all these strangers in my nakedness and disarray. My accuser said to Jesus in a stern voice, teacher, this woman was caught in the very act of adultery. The Law of Moses commands that we stone such women to death. What do you say that we should do? I am evil but I am not stupid. I could see exactly how these men were trying to trap Jesus. The preacher took several moments looking from face to face in the group of men and also focusing his penetrating eyes on me too. Without uttering a word of reply, Jesus went down on one knee and began writing on the dirt in the road with his finger. I could not see clearly what he was writing but it seemed to be names of people. When he was finished, he stood and again looked around the group who had restrained me. Finally, he said in a calm but flat voice, let the one among you who is without sin of his own cast the first stone at this woman. Having said that, Jesus once again bent down and wrote something next to each name he had previously traced. One by one, starting with the most senior members of the group, they approached Jesus and observed what he had written in the dirt. Again it was not easy for me to read the words but each man appeared stunned to see what Jesus had written opposite his name. After seeing the words in the dirt, the men turned and began walking away. This whole episode took perhaps five minutes. At the end of this time, I was left standing near Jesus all by myself. We stood facing each other. I was still trembling from the recent trauma I had experienced. He was expressionless. After several moments, he said to me, Mosha, where have all your accusers gone? It looks like no one is left. All I could think to say was, no one, sir. Again there was a moment of silence. Finally, Jesus said to me, neither do I condemn you, Mosha. Go now and sin no more. Following those words, Jesus gently smiled at me, turned and left the square.

I now found myself completely alone in the temple square. I walked over to the stairs leading to the temple and sat down. I re-arranged my clothes to cover my nakedness and began to reflect on what had just happened to me. I was used to entrap Jesus. No wonder I had felt wariness last night when that potential client approached me. His job was to lead me into an adulterous situation. He was part of the mob that abducted me and hauled me away to the temple square. Jesus was too clever for them. I got up and walked over to where Jesus had written in the dirt. There were the names of the men who captured me, and next to each name was written a grave sin. Jesus had known what was in their heart of hearts and silently accused them of their own offenses against God. I now understand why they walked away from the scene without further comment after reading what he wrote.

As I continued to reflect about my encounter with Jesus, I was struck by two things. First, I never thanked him for what he done. Had I become that ungrateful and cynical? I was really sorry that I had failed to indicate my appreciation to Jesus. Second, he had told me to go and sin no more. But, he had never told me that my past sins were forgiven. Did he expect me to return immediately to my life of degradation? If I did decide to redirect my life, how could I seek pardon for my past behavior? I felt that his rescue of me, and the few words he spoke, were intended to modify the direction of my life. But, was it possible to change? I knew nothing else. I sat on the steps pondering what to do next while I began arguing with myself. What do you mean that you can't do anything else? Of course you can do other things! You can wash clothes or scrub floors or work in the fields to earn a living. You are deluding yourself to think that selling your body is the only way to live. Wake up, woman! You can change if you really want to change. Back and forth I went considering what a radical change would mean compared to returning to the familiar prostitution. It finally dawned on me that this Jesus had offered me one last chance to amend my life. He had saved me from possible death and refused to judge my past. It was now or never, I concluded. I arose from the steps and walked away leaving the temple square behind and leaving my old life behind too. I vowed to start anew.

Few of us live like Mosha. We acknowledge that all are sinners, but only a handful of folks lead totally reprehensible lives. Whether we are great or small sinners we all need "The Four Cs" to get back on the right track:

- *<u>Contrition</u>. Nothing happens until we turn our back on sin and show true sorrow.*
- *<u>Conversion</u>. We must sincerely commit to amending our lives.*
- *<u>Confession</u>. We must openly speak the words about our past sins especially to those we have sinned against.*
- *<u>Celebration</u>. In thanksgiving for forgiveness, we appreciate the graces we have received.*

Unfortunately, much of the world is in denial about the reality of sin and evil. Things that previously caused shame and embarrassment are shrugged off as "the way things are now." While that is sad, it does not mean that you and I have to participate in this obfuscation. Let's not kid ourselves: the battle against sinfulness in our lives is a never-ending fight. Remember, with God's grace and your own determination, you can win. Let's all start today.

JOBAL, THE CRIPPLED MAN AT BETHESDA
John 5: 1 – 18

I suppose you think I like to sit here by the pool at Bethesda. Well, you would be wrong about my preference for faithful attendance here. This place is also called the House of Mercy. I can't imagine why. I find no mercy here. I have come here virtually every day since I was ten years old. That is thirty-eight years ago and I am sick and tired of spending my time with about three thousand other folks who are blind, deaf, lame, crippled or can't walk, like me. There is no one camping out here daily who is not deformed or sick or crazy. Do you think we enjoy enduring endless frustration as we try to use the supposedly curative waters of the pool to become whole again? Frankly, I don't know why I continue to come. You would think after all these years I might have learned my cure is not just a few feet away. Instead my hope for wholeness is probably a world away, as far as the earth is from the moon. But habits and routines are hard to break so here I am today and I will probably be here tomorrow too, just like all the rest.

As a youngster, it was obvious that I had been born with a serious defect to my back, hips and legs that made walking impossible. My parents did their best to care for me but everyone knew that I was not going to be cured. All the religious people in the Jerusalem community believed that angels of God visited the pool at Bethesda daily and could cure the most terrible infirmities. Legend was that an angel came to the pool at random times and disturbed the waters. Many believed that the first person who reached the water after the angel had broken the surface calm would be cured. When there is no human solution to an intractable problem, many will turn to reliance upon miracles even in the face of contradictory evidence. Did I believe I might be cured in this miraculous way? I did believe there was an Almighty God, but I was seriously doubtful that some agitated water would be the source of my ability to walk. And yet, back I came day after day.

As I mentioned, many people come here daily, perhaps three thousand, I estimate. Surprisingly the area adjacent to the pool is quite comfortable. There are five large porticos, or porches, that surround the water and each one is covered so that everyone is shaded from the mid-day sun. Being a long-term daily visitor, I know many of the others who come here as well. Generous people in the community provide us with water and a little food each day. We are grateful for their thoughtfulness. I find it interesting that certain people always seem to position themselves on the same porch each day. It is like a seat in the temple; everyone claims a particular spot. A large number of the people at Bethesda are transient. There are new faces seen each day and old ones disappear never to return. To pass the time, we regulars gossip about the comings and goings and speculate regarding the type of problems the new people are experiencing. Often there is no indication that an angel has come today to rile the waters. At other times, I will hear a shout and then observe many people frantically trying to get into the water first from their porch. I can tell you honestly that during my years of attending the pool, I have never personally seen any miraculous cures that tradition promotes. I am not saying no one has ever been cured. I merely comment that I haven't seen such a thing with my own eyes. I admit that I have observed the dead calm water suddenly shimmer because of some surface agitation. At such times I have desperately crawled or rolled toward the water praying that I might be the first to touch it. I have never come close. There are always others younger and faster. I don't think I have a chance.

It is probably true that most of us do not deserve to be healed in the first place. I can tell you from firsthand knowledge that many of us sitting on the porches have not led very exemplary lives, From what I have heard, the regulars at Bethesda represent a large cross section of sinners, guilty of leading sinful lives. Just because we appear to be physically handicapped or defective, you should definitely not conclude we are a collection of poor, innocent castoffs from society. On the contrary, our band is comprised of murderers, rapists, thieves, robbers and miscreants of many stripes. We whine and repeat our hard luck stories to one another, lounging around the pool at Bethesda indulging our sloth and laziness. Being here is easy and relatively comfortable. We eat, drink and gossip while waiting for someone else to rescue us from a life of misery. Most of us have little interest in doing much to help ourselves.

Many of the regulars at the pool are indifferent to the latest political or religious gossip. That's because we see no benefit to us personally from such an involvement. On a Sabbath day, I was in my usual spot when I noticed a commotion at a distant porch. A tall, handsome young man had entered the area followed by a small handful of followers. He was mingling with the people and stopped to have extended conversations with some. I watched this from my perch wondering who this man was and what he wanted. The man and his entourage were headed my way. I called out to those around me, but none of them could identify him. Finally, he reached my place and halted, looking at me intently. He made small talk asking my name and how long I had been visiting the pool. Then he said a most remarkable thing to me. Jobal, do you want to be well? Initially, his question annoyed me. I found it to be the stupidest thing I had ever heard. Of course, I want to be well! Why do you think I've been sitting by this damn pool for thirty-eight years? The words exploded in my brain but not out of my mouth. I restrained myself

Greg Hadley

and cautiously said to him, sir, I have no one to help me get to the water when it is stirred up by the angel. Others always get there before me, I told him. He paused, looking at me seriously, and then said to me, Jobal, get up, pick up your mat and walk out of here. You are well. I sat there momentarily, stunned by what this man had said. I had never gotten up before without the aid of my crutches but he had told me to get up. Warily, I got on my knees and, with the help of my hands, I pushed myself to a crouch and then a standing position. I could not believe it! This was a miracle! I could walk! The other people on the porch looked at me disbelieving, some with terror in their eyes for what they had just witnessed. I felt giddy and light-headed as I took some tentative initial steps. The man who had cured me just lightly patted me on the back and moved on, leaving my porch and heading for the temple area. I still had no idea who this man was. He had cured my life-long disfigurement, but I did not know his name.

I picked up my mat and started walking toward an exit from the pool area. I was amazed how steady my gait was; I was having no difficulty at all. Just as I was about to leave the porch, I was blocked by a temple official. He sternly said to me, don't you know it is the Sabbath? You are not permitted to carry a mat on this day. I relayed my story to the official telling him that the man who cured me had directed that I take my mat and walk away. Even more sternly, the official asked me, who is this man who told you to break the Sabbath laws by carrying your mat? I told the official honestly, I do not know the man, and I do not see him in the vicinity. Please leave me alone. I am only doing what I was told by the man who cured my deformity. The official angrily let me pass out of the area.

I wasn't sure where I should go. Although I am not a religious man, I felt it would be appropriate to visit the temple and offer a prayer of thanksgiving for my cure. After all, I had never thanked the man personally for what he had done for me. At least, I could thank Almighty God. I entered the temple and proceeded to the unfamiliar outer court. The area was full of people praying, reading scripture and buying and selling small sacrificial offerings. I was startled by a tap on my shoulder. Turning, I was face to face with the man who cured me. He said to me in a kind and gentle voice, my name is Jesus. I know about your past. Your life has seen its share of sinfulness. I cured you on the porch today because I wanted to give you a second chance to live a productive and righteous life. I have made you well. Amend your life and sin no more or something worse may happen to you. Do you understand, he asked? I stammered my thanks to Jesus and promised my life would change. I turned away for just a second. When I turned back, Jesus had disappeared. I said my little prayer of thanks to God and started heading home. Once again, I encountered the same temple official that I had seen at Bethesda. He threatened me once more about the mat being carried on the Sabbath. I did tell him that I had discovered the name of the person who had cured me. The official seemed very eager to have that information. He pulled a piece of paper out of his tunic and scribbled furiously when I told him that Jesus of Nazareth had made me whole after thirty-eight years being crippled.

The transition back to normal life after sitting by the pool all those years was not as easy as I expected. I had acquired some very bad habits of laziness and dependence on others. I fell back into bad behavior a few times, but I sincerely worked at amending my life as I had promised Jesus I would. I followed his activities for the rest of his human life and now do my best to be faithful to The Way as preached by his disciples. I heard Jesus say one thing that I will never forget: come to me, all you are burdened and I will give you rest, for my yoke is easy and my burden is light. Whenever things get difficult for me, I remember these words of Jesus.

Although subtle, there is some correlation between Jobal and his sick or disfigured friends with you and me. It is a sad fact that many of us today continue to attend our churches regularly but never experience a true conversion. How does it happen that the saving graces of the Holy Spirit only put a small dent on our souls? Even daily prayer leaves us with pious words in our mouths but not much real change in our lives. We ask sincerely, why can't I make a connection with God? What is holding me back from living a life full of love, peace, joy, trust in God, and service to others? Consider these five reasons, please. First, you and I may be too sick to really turn our lives around. Why? Our sins, even little ones, can be very incapacitating to us. Second, you and I may be too weak. Our sins can leave us without any energy to make needed changes. Third, you and I may be blind. If so, we may not be able to discern the difference between right and wrong. Fourth, we may be lame making it very difficult for us to walk uprightly. Finally, our limbs may have withered and atrophied. That can paralyze any effort you or I make to improve our spiritual lives. Jobal was chosen from many to experience the miraculous and healing touch of Jesus. Why Jobal and not someone else? We will probably never know. Just like Jobal and all the others who attended the pool at Bethesda we are members of Christian communities that are full of sick, weak, blind, lame and paralyzed people. While we lack the infinite healing touch of Jesus, we should ask God to let us be His arms and legs so that we can be of healing service to all our brothers and sisters in the Body of Christ.

If we are effective in doing God's work in this way, our personal face-to-face encounter with Jesus the Christ will be as memorable for us as it was for Jobal in our story.

MAXIS, WHO MADE THE CROWN OF THORNS
Matthew 27: 29
Mark 15: 17
John 19: 2, 5

I am a common Roman soldier, garrisoned in Jerusalem for almost two years. My home is in a small town near Rome. Being a soldier is my job. I have learned how to deal with the good and the bad of military life. For example, always expect the worst in people. Except for my mother, all people hate soldiers. My comrades and I protect and defend each other, but we assume all others want to make our lives as miserable as possible. Many of my mates are brutish animals although I expect them to watch my back just as I watch theirs. While I am a young man, I have become cynical and distrustful of all strangers I meet. My assumption is that they would cut my heart out without remorse, so I view everyone as a potential deadly threat. I have also learned it is wise to deal out pain to others before they have the opportunity to inflict it on you. This attitude probably fuels the hatred the people of this country have for Romans. Frankly, I could care less. I equally despise the Jews, especially their mealy mouthed religious leaders who would lie about anything if it helped to save their own power or skin. I am looking forward to the day when I am ordered to keep some of these so-called leaders in line. That is the day I will teach them what physical agony is all about. I can hardly wait for that day to arrive because I am very good at my job.

The Roman army seems firmly in control in this godforsaken land. We have plenty of soldiers and any hint of civil disorder is harshly dealt with by our troops. Yet, there always seems to be some new social or religious volcano erupting somewhere, especially around

Jerusalem. Recently, our commander has been telling us about a Jewish religious leader who has been stirring up the people. While this man is from the north in Galilee, we are told he is now on the way here to celebrate some Jew festival. Those people are always having some kind of religious feast; I can't keep them straight. I think the current one is called Passover. I have no idea what it is all about. Anyway, this guy who is potential trouble is named Jesus of Nazareth. He would be smart to put a lid on his boiling pot or he could be very sorry. Our bosses will not stand for any unrest or civil disobedience around here. If this man or his followers step out of line, there will be a few cracked heads, believe you me. My mates and I know how to deal out punishment to anyone not obeying our orders.

I was on duty Thursday night in the palace of the Procurator, Pontius Pilate. He is the highest-ranking Roman official in Israel and is responsible for all the big and final decisions about ruling this land. I had seen Pilate at work a few times—he is ruthless—but, as a mere soldier, I had never spoken to him. The Jewish leaders had descended on the palace this evening, dragging with them the man Jesus I told you about. The Jews were screaming to Pilate sitting on his judge's bench that Jesus deserved death for his statements about being the king of the Jews. Pilate was told that claim made Jesus appear the equal of Caesar, so Pilate was obliged to eradicate Jesus. As usual, there was a lot of yelling between all the parties, but my mates and I really didn't care about all these legal positions. We knew it was our job to protect Roman property and authority. We intended to do our job if called upon by our commander.

While all this was going on, I was positioned just a few feet away from Jesus. He was tall and stood stoically while the turmoil roiled about him. His hands were restrained behind his back. It was obvious he had already taken a few blows to the head. One cheek and eye were puffy and purple and blood was trickling out of the corner of his mouth. He hadn't seen anything yet, I thought to myself. Normally, I like people the Jews hate. It's like the old saying: the enemy of my enemy is my friend. But, this Jesus must have caused a lot of trouble. I could tell by just looking around at all the frantic activity in Pilate's courtyard. People who cause trouble need to be taught a lesson. I was just waiting for the word and I would be happy to do my part to show Jesus a thing or two.

While all the discussion continued, Jesus began to look around at the people nearby. He made eye contact with me. For some reason, he smiled at me. Did he think I was his friend? Just to let him know where he stood, I spit on him. He said to me, have I done something to you? I snapped back at him, you've been causing problems. I don't like people who cause problems. Jesus responded, I have only asked people to love one another, follow God's rules for life and be kind. The trouble has been caused by those who don't like to hear these words, he added. I didn't have the patience to argue with Jesus. The only reason I needed to hate him was the fact that he was a Jew.

Pilate continued his awkward negotiations with the Jewish leaders about Jesus' fate. Soon a decision was reached. Pilate ordered that Jesus be scourged and then delivered to the high priest for final disposition. One of my mates said, we'll see how the king of the Jews likes the cat-o-nine tails whip. Hearing that, I laughingly said, our king ought to have a crown, don't you think? I went outside the courtyard and found a thorn bush. Using my knife, I carefully cut a section about three feet long. The branches were still green so they were pliable. Ouch! One of the thorns stuck me. I cursed in anger at the pain. I grabbed a pair of metal tongs used to put charcoal in the heating braziers found in the courtyard area. There was a small round pedestal nearby and, using the tongs, I pulled the thorn branch segment into a circle. I was pleased with my handiwork; it looked just like a crown for a king. My comrades were amusing themselves by mocking Jesus. Hail, king of the Jews, one called out. I walked over to Jesus holding the crown made of thorns with the tongs. I placed the crown on his head and used a couple of hard hits with the side of the tongs to force the thorns into Jesus' skull. Blood spurted from the wounds on his scalp. Looking at me through pain and distress, Jesus said, my young friend, I am sure you did not intend to injure me maliciously. You were just joining your fellow soldiers in having some fun at my expense. I preach love toward all and that includes you. I forgive you for what you have just done to me.

These words from the Jew made me feel very uncomfortable. Usually, when I use force on someone, they shriek in pain and curse me for what I have just done to them. Often this is my reward. This man said he forgave me. What kind of a person would do something like that? I immediately lost my taste for further participation in this violation of Jesus. Let others scourge, mutilate and humiliate him. Something had just happened to me that compelled me to go outside the courtyard. Once in the nearby street, I violently vomited the contents of my stomach, and more it seemed. I was mortified by my own actions. Had I suddenly gone soft and lost my nerve? I hated what this man Jesus had done to me. Somehow, he reached inside of me and tore my soul in half. No, that is not right, I thought. What he had done was let me see deeply into my own soul. I did not like what I saw. Jesus was preaching love while I was used to practicing hate. He said words of forgiveness while I was disrespecting him. Ideas darted throughout my brain. Formerly, so sure of myself and my views, I was now completely confused and conflicted about the basic concepts of right and wrong. Can a person change direction in life so profoundly after just one brief encounter with another? My brain had turned to mush.

I later heard from my friends how Jesus had been violently scourged into a bloody pulp. The next day my comrades led him outside the city gates and crucified him. The stories were told to me by men who relished the agony they had imposed on Jesus. They shrugged off their sinister violence with boasts and laughter as they recalled the pain they had inflicted on this Jew. Noticing my somber reaction to their stories, one soldier said to me, what's wrong with you, Maxis? I had no idea what to answer.

Something dreadful has happened in the last thirty years with the way people interact with one another. It used to be that people could have a serious and respectful discussion about issues where they held completely opposite views. The talk might become heated but seldom did you see massive incivility and bitter contention as you do today. What has happened to make society so polarized on a whole host of issues? I have heard others say, I just can't stand that person; his thinking is defective and his logic so appalling I can't have a reasonable discussion with him. Should I have expected anything different? After all, you know he is a...(you fill in the missing word: Democrat; Republican; Jew; Catholic; Protestant; Muslim; Black; Gay; on food stamps and welfare; a foreigner; any other pejorative term that comes to mind). God forbid that you or I would ever mouth words like that, right? Have we thought something like that? Be honest with yourself. Our minds seem to shut down when we hear the position of the other side on almost every social and political issue of the day. Whose fault is it that we cannot seem to have a calm exchange of views about things like abortion, tax fairness, government involvement in health care, education or poverty programs, race equality, the proper care of the environment, religious dogma, same sex unions or marriage, the international community of nations or economic principles?

Could it be our fault—yours and mine? Have we so shut down our willingness to listen to different points of view and have some empathy for the deeply held ideas and passions of others? As the cartoon character Pogo memorialized: we have met the enemy, and they are us. It was one lesson Maxis learned in this story.

REUBEN, MARTHA AND THEIR SON, SHEM, A MAN BLIND FROM BIRTH
John 9: 1 – 40

(Two stories are presented to you. You will hear from Reuben and Martha, the parents of a man born blind who received the gift of sight in adulthood. Then, the son of the couple, Shem, will tell his story about the remarkable events that led to his cure. Unfortunately the parents and son are estranged, thus requiring two narratives so you can understand the full story. First, the parents speak.)

I am Reuben. I will speak for my wife, Martha, and me. She doesn't like to get involved in this sort of thing. Besides, she is quite emotional about the relationship with our son, Shem. I'm concerned she might break down if she told you how she felt about this situation. Anyway, I know exactly what is in her heart, so the story I will tell accurately describes how we both view the recent events.

We try to mind our own business. In exchange for not poking into other people's lives, we want to be left alone by them. That way we avoid all the idle gossip in the neighborhood and stay detached from the meaningless drama so many people love to generate. All this stuff about being involved in your community seems like an excuse for being a busybody. So, we stay pretty much to ourselves and appreciate it when others reciprocate. Unfortunately, not too many people share this view of life.

To make a long story short, Shem is now twenty-eight years old. From the day he was born, he was a burden to our family. We knew right away that there was something dreadfully wrong with his eyes. Several months after birth we expected that his eyes would begin focusing on objects. That didn't happen, and when he reached about one year old we were quite sure he had been born blind. Of course, all in the community are quick to believe that when God curses your family this way it must be due to some terrible sin that the parents have committed in the past. Neighbors start to look at you differently, and you can't avoid the whispered rumors about what might have caused the blindness. Martha and I hated that. We felt blameless but no one would have believed that even if we told them.

You have to be pretty callous not to love your own child even though he might be physically defective. We did our best to love and care for Shem as he grew up, but he was not very lovable at any stage of the maturing process. He was a terrible whiner, and always complained about his defect to all who would listen. He was brooding, selfish and angry most of the time—who could blame him? Worst of all, as he reached adulthood, he constantly pointed to us as the source of all his misery. His insistent negative outlook on life, and on us, created a deep chasm between him and his mother and me. I admit it; we gave up on him and were happy when he finally left our home to become a beggar near the temple.

There wasn't much contact with Shem after that. Oh, once in awhile we would see him when we went to temple on Sabbath, but all our conversations were very strained and awkward. This went on for several years. One day, a close neighbor came to our home to tell us an amazing story. He had been in the temple area today and saw someone who looked almost exactly like Shem. Except, our neighbor said, the man he saw had perfect eyesight. As a matter of fact, several neighbors told us the identical story. The person they saw certainly looked like Shem but he could see and such a thing could not have happened to our son...could it? The multiple stories were so curious that we traveled down to the temple area to seek out Shem. As we found our son, he was surrounded with agitated temple officials and other religious leaders.

We were absolutely stunned to see that our boy could apparently see. The elders were pressing Shem. How were your eyes opened, they demanded? Shem explained what a man named Jesus had done to him. We heard the people scoffing at this and stating that Jesus had violated the Sabbath laws. The Jewish leaders asked Shem, where is this Jesus? Shem answered, I don't know where he is. Several of the Jews were from our temple and they recognized us. They turned to us and said, isn't this your son? You have told us that he was born blind. How is it that he can now see? Both Martha and I felt we were now on dangerous ground. We didn't want to be expelled from our temple, and we were unsure of the facts about our son's sight. I said to the leaders, this is our son and we can testify that he has been blind since his birth. We have absolutely no idea how he now sees nor do we know who opened his eyes. Martha then spoke up and said, why don't you ask Shem for this information? After all, he is of age and can certainly speak for himself. Both Martha and I were wary about attributing any miraculous power to this itinerant preacher Jesus. We planned to continue living in this community. We had no intention of upsetting the Jewish leaders. We knew they could make our life miserable if we did.

While we were happy for Shem, we left the area as soon as we could. Neighbors told us later that the Jews continued to question our son and the back-and-forth discussion became quite contentious. One of our friends told us that he had stayed around to see what transpired. He reported that we would have been proud of Shem since he really stood his ground against the leaders and never seemed intimidated by their demands for more information. Martha and I didn't say much to each other that evening. We both were having a difficult time processing everything we had seen and heard and understanding what it meant to Shem and to us. I said to

Martha, we should make an effort at reconciliation with Shem. While she nodded her agreement, I did not sense that she believed reconciliation would ever happen.

(It is now Shem's turn to give his version of the story.)

I know you have already heard from my parents. It's really not worth trying to dispute their view of my growing up years. I admit I was a difficult case for them until I left home. It is also true that my bitterness and anger overflowed toward them even when they didn't deserve it. I'm sorry that I didn't do a better job of reaching out to them or attempting to be reconciled. I guess I just didn't have the emotional maturity to make that happen. Well, that is all past now. Perhaps the future between my parents and me can be more cordial and loving. I'm not sure of that, but I do promise to make an effort once I fully absorb the stupendous events that have just taken place in my life. Can you fully understand the magnitude of the following statement? I spent the first twenty-eight years of my life totally blind, never able to see light. In a few moments, my life was changed by a stranger who gave sight to my eyes. Has something as profound ever happened to you? I'm guessing your answer is no.

It all began one day while I was begging by the side of the road. Although sightless, my other senses are pretty acute. I heard a small group of people pass my spot on the road. One voice said, Rabbi Jesus, is this beggar blind because of his own sins or the sins of his parents? A gentle but powerful voice responded, neither he nor his parents sinned. He is blind so that the work of God might be made visible through him. The one they called Jesus then said, I have to do my Father's work while it is still day. Nighttime is coming when no one will be able to work. So, while I am still here I will be the light of the world to all people. At that, I heard someone come close to me, kneel down and spit. A few seconds later, a pair of very gentle hands placed a round piece of mud about the size of a Roman coin on each of my eyes. I felt like a mere bystander. I had not asked for anything and had only a vague idea what had just happened. The voice of the Jesus then said to me, go and wash the mud off your eyes in the Pool of Siloam. The pool was nearby and one of my friends guided me to it. As instructed, I washed the mud away. When I did as I was told, something incredible took place—I could see! For the first time in my life, my eyes sent information to my brain about colors, shapes, people and all the world around me. I rushed back to the spot where Jesus put mud on me. But he was not there. Of course, I was enthusiastically telling friends and strangers alike what had just happened to me. I can see! For the first time in my life, I can see!

People who said they were friends of my parents seemed curious when they saw me. I told them what had happened to me and that a Rabbi named Jesus had given me my sight. I heard one man say, he certainly looks like Shem but it can't be since we know he has been blind since birth. Things like that just cannot be fixed. One of my friends brought me to the Pharisees and other Jewish leaders. I told them my story but they didn't believe me. One Pharisee said to me, this Jesus cannot be from God because we know he does not keep the Sabbath. Still others offered, how can a sinful man do such signs? There was a lot of disagreement and discord among these leaders. Finally, one of them turned to me and said, what do you have to say about Jesus since he opened your eyes? I thought about the question for a moment and finally responded, I believe Jesus is a prophet.

As you already know, my parents showed up to see what had happened and the Pharisees questioned them as well. I could hear the nervousness in their voices and see discomfort in their body language as they were examined by the Pharisees. It was obvious to me that they didn't want to get involved. They probably worried about being shunned by the temple if they said anything good about Jesus. They were correct about that too. I have to admit it would have been nice to hear them praising God for the wondrous miracle that cured my blindness. Oh, well, I guess I need to be more understanding of my parents.

After haranguing my parents, the Pharisees decided to go after me again. The first thing they said to me was, give God the praise! That's Hebrew idiom for "tell the truth!" They started out by saying, we know this Jesus is a sinner. Just look how he violates the Sabbath. I shot back at them, I don't know if he is a sinner or not. What I do know is that I was blind and now I can see. Once again they demanded, what did he do to you to cure your blindness? I answered them sarcastically, I already told you what Jesus did. Do you want to hear my story again? Maybe you are so intrigued that you wish to become his disciples, is that right? I could see that made them furious. They all yelled and ridiculed me saying, you are that man's disciple. As for us, we are the disciples of Moses. We know God spoke to Moses but we have no idea where Jesus comes from. Laughing at them I said, it is amazing that you do not know where Jesus is from but you admit he opened my eyes. I continued, I don't think God listens to sinners. He only helps those who are devout and love God. As far as I know no one like me, blind from birth, has ever had his sight restored. If this man were not from God, I don't believe he could have cured me. My words angered the Pharisees even more. One shouted at me, your blindness from birth was caused by your sinfulness. And you are trying to teach us? Get out of here, you sinful and arrogant man! With that, the mob grabbed me and physically led me away from the temple square.

I wasn't hurt but I was shaken by the violent reaction of the Jewish leaders. My breathing was shallow and labored as I left the temple. As I worked to gain my composure, I saw Jesus walking toward me. He was solicitous of my condition and said to me, Shem, are you all right? Yes, Rabbi, I am feeling better but I am glad to get away from those riotous men. Jesus looked at me intently for a moment and then asked me a strange question. He said, do you believe in the Son of Man? I wasn't sure how to answer. The term, Son of Man, was used to denote the Messiah. That I did know. After pausing for a moment I responded, who is he, sir, that I might believe in him? Jesus looked deeply into my eyes and said, you have seen him and the one speaking with you is he. For the second time this day, I was disbelieving. The promised Messiah was standing in front of me? I blurted out to Jesus, I do believe Lord. At that, I dropped to my knees and worshipped him. Jesus moved closer and put his hand on my shoulder. As he did so, a few of the Pharisees exited the temple area and were walking towards us. Jesus then said to me, I came into the world for judgment so that those who were blind might see and those who do see might become blind. These words of Jesus were overheard by the approaching Pharisees. One of them mockingly said to Jesus, you are not calling us blind are you? Turning toward them Jesus said, if you were blind you would have no sin but now you are telling me you see just fine. Therefore, your sin remains with you.

Following this exchange, the Pharisees went on their way and Jesus took his leave too. His final words to me were as follows: Shem, you have received two blessings this day. I ask that you use both of them to help build up the kingdom of God. I will pray for you, Shem. Now go in peace. With that, Jesus departed.

There were many things in my life that needed amendment. I tried to follow the advice Jesus had given to me. I found it wasn't as easy as I thought it would be. It is hard for a sinner like me to turn things around. But, Jesus did inspire me to try and that's what I am doing. Next on my agenda is figuring out how to recreate a loving relationship with my mother and father. That will be hard.

It seems appropriate to me that the last story in this book focuses on Jesus as the light of the world. In our day-to-day lives, we encounter so many shades of gray. It is often difficult to sort out what is the moral, just, fair and loving thing to do. We are forced to make so many nuanced decisions every day. Our clouded, human minds cannot always sort out the pros and cons of each situation we face in a neat and decisive way. We struggle with relationships, especially with family. We wonder how we should tell the truth without offending a loved one. We yearn for clear political options and find there may be some truth on both sides. Every difficult choice we face presents several forks in the road. Even after finally reaching a decision, we second-guess ourselves, wondering if we are doing the right thing. Yes, our lives are full of gray, dark gray and black. It is only when we turn to Jesus, the Light of the World, for his guidance and grace that we can be at peace with our choices. Our Lord shines his light for us on the shadowy roads we travel each day. We have seen in all the stories of this book that the main character often left the encounter with Jesus a little conflicted and not quite sure about what was to come. As I wrote in the Preface, we have the advantage of knowing how the Gospel stories turned out. Let's all take advantage of that fact and let the Light of the World guide us as we walk along the path of our salvation journey.

ABOUT THE AUTHOR

Greg Hadley with his wife, Evelyn, lives in Lake Oswego, Oregon in a retirement community. The couple has six children and fourteen grandchildren.

After completing his undergraduate education at the University of San Francisco, finishing his MBA studies at Pepperdine University, and attending the Harvard Business School, Greg spent his professional life in the business world. He worked for IBM and was General Manager of Computer Sciences of Australia. Then, for twenty years, Hadley and his partners acquired, operated and sold industrial companies. Moving from California to Oregon in 1990 Greg established a management consulting practice, spent time as a college educator, author, and professional public speaker. Greg also spends time in civic, political and community volunteer activities.

Hadley spent thirty-nine years as an amateur baseball umpire, mostly at the NCAA Division 1 level. He has authored six previous books prior to this one. Please see the list of titles at the beginning of this book. For further information, visit the website www.gbhadley.com.

Made in the USA
San Bernardino, CA
27 January 2018